Gossip

The Biography of a Yacht

Cecily Gould

By the Same Author

The Living Rivier 1972
A Tapestry of Time 2001

Gossip

The Biography of a Yacht

By Cecily Gould

Illustrated

Seafarer Books

2003

© Cecily Gould 2003

First published in the UK by:-
Gentry Books 1972

This edition by:-
Seafarer Books
102 Redwald Road
Rendlesham
Woodbridge
Suffolk IP12 2TE

UK ISBN 0 9542750 0 4

Typesetting and design by Julie Beadle
Cover design by Louis Mackay
Photographs by family and Yacht Shop
arranged by Louis Mackay

British Library Cataloguing in Publication Data
Gould, Cecily
  Gossip. – 2nd ed.
  1. Gossip (Yacht) 2. Voyages and travels 3. Yachting
  I. Title
  910. 4'5'0904

  ISBN 0954275004

Printed in Finland by W. S. Bookwell OY

For Dambom

Introduction and Acknowledgements

One of the most enjoyable aspects of writing *Gossip*'s biography has been the discovery of how helpful everyone, without exception, has been in answering my many questions. The Royal Ocean Racing Club, the Royal Yachting Association, The Island Sailing Club, Rolls-Royce Ltd, Mr. Henry Knowler and Mr. Cecil Atkey have all contributed in this way. For help and encouragement, I would like to thank Admiral Sir Manley Power, K.C.B., C.B.E., D.S.O., Joan Sebborn, Ian Parsons, Juliet O'Hea, and Bryen and Sadie Gentry. Also, many members of my family, especially my mother, my sisters Bess and Lucia, my brother Alan, my cousin Ronald Saxby, my son James and, above all, Dambom, whose ability to recapture his early days in sail endowed me from my childhood with a love and fascination for *Gossip* and the sea.

William Borel for the photographs and the account of *Gossip*'s last voyage, Richard Heming for the photograph of the painting of *Gossip* on the cover, the photograph of Anthea and Marion Heming for the photograph of the author with the model of *Gossip* in the Royal Solent Yacht Club, Beken of Cowes, Harold Hayles, Mrs. Abson and James Gould. For the picture of *Gossip* on the jacket, Derek Foster and for the sketch of Dambom on the back, Professor Janos Jakuba.

Monsieur Berthier for his account of 'Old Ships' and the charming sketches of *Gossip* and her interior. My brother-in-law, Lionel Landon, for his translation of this article. The Society of Authors as the literary representative of the estate of John Masefield for permission to quote from 'Sea Fever'.

Contents

Illustrations

Maps at end of book
1. Scandinavian Voyage
2. English Channel and Brittany

Photo Section

Dambom aged five
Cecily and Jay on the river Yar in Tigger
Jay (Lucia), Cecily and Dambom on Mount Vesuvius
Gossip at Berg on the Göta Canal. Bess (left) and Cecily (right)
Anthea up for the scrub at Yarmouth quay
Sailing *Anthea*
Cecily's marriage to Sir Basil Gould
Dambom at the wheel of *Gossip*
Fitting out *Anthea* at Yarmouth quay
William Borel sailing *Gossip* with the long tiller.
Cecily, as a guest aboard *Gossip*
The author in 2002, in the Royal Solent Yacht Club.
The model of *Gossip* was made for Dambom by Cecily's cousin, Ronald Saxby.

Prologue

She sailed out of the harbour in the soft evening light of autumn, the sun lighting her varnished mast, a dark green yacht, gaff rigged and sturdy, all her white canvas set. At her masthead fluttered a banner with a strange device, over her stern the tricolour of France.

I watched from the quay with my father and my two sisters as she sailed out of our lives for ever. No one spoke and at last we turned away. She had been part of our lives for over forty years. What tales she could tell, how intimately she knew us all. At that moment I decided to tell her story, not a spectacular tale of great endeavours but a collection of memories of the fun and the adventures of an ordinary family in an ordinary yacht.

1880 - Dambom

My father, known to his family and friends as 'Dambom', is a small wiry man of superhuman strength and energy, consisting almost entirely of bone and muscle and fitted with some sort of sparking mechanism, which is the nearest thing to perpetual motion that I have ever seen. He has a Puck-like sense of humour and a great affection for his family.

Tom Kelloway, a local boat-builder who could sum up anyone in a single sentence, said of him, ' 'e may be a little man but 'e always takes the 'eavy end.'

Even now in his ninety-first year he still races his Yarmouth One Design (Y.O.D.) *Anthea* at Cowes, and reduces vast trees to firewood as a winter hobby besides doing all the work in a large, rambling garden.

He expects us all to keep pace with him, especially his three daughters, and we were brought up, if not to take the 'eavy end, at least to take one end, and so it was that as small girls we were to be seen at one end of the big cross-cut saw, or clutching a paint brush or scraper when it came to fitting out the boat. Outside help was never welcomed and on the rare occasions when it was offered he would reply, 'The girls and I can manage.'

His first recollection of sailing is when, as a boy of fifteen, he was staying at Kirkwall in the Orkneys. One morning two of his fellow guests asked him to come sailing with them in a little fishing boat they had hired for the day. Full of interest and enthusiasm he followed the men down to the harbour and boarded the boat which was lying alongside the quay. They were soon busy hoisting the sails and coiling up the ropes and as they cast off one of the men casually handed him the tiller and told him to take her out of the harbour. Dambom had never steered a boat before but didn't like to admit it in case someone took the helm from him. Gingerly he pushed the tiller first one way, then the other until he grasped the principle of the thing, then looking, or trying to look as if he had steered all his life, he took the boat through the entrance and out to the open sea. Fate was on his side, as it so often seemed to be in later years, for the wind was free and he didn't have to bother about keeping to windward. After a short time one of the men took the helm from him and he was able to observe and learn without displaying his ignorance.

He didn't sail again until he was seventeen, when, after the death of his parents he came to live with his Great Aunt Bessy at Freshwater in the Isle of Wight. This venerable old lady, widowed in the Crimean War, played an important part in Dambom's early development. It was to her house that he came as a boy whenever his parents paused on their incessant travels. It was here that he made his first garden. She also inspired him to collect wild flowers, which she hand-painted most exquisitely in a book which contained most of the flora found in the British Isles by the time she died in 1910 at the age of ninety-five.

It was during one of these early visits while walking
on the Freshwater downs searching for butterflies
that, as a boy of six, Dambom met his great aunt's
friend and contemporary Alfred Tennyson. After a
brief introduction the small boy politely excused
himself and continued to chase the chalk-hill blue
butterfly which he considered of more importance
than the elderly bearded poet shrouded in a large
black hat and flowing cloak.

The popular boats at the time when Dambom came
to live in Freshwater, were the small clinker-built
Solent Seabirds, based in Yarmouth, and it was in
one of these little boats that he mastered the first
steps in sailing and seamanship. He sailed as often as
he could that first summer but never cared for the
racing. He preferred to navigate and explore the
many creeks and rivers of the Solent.

Up to this time Dambom had never known a proper
home as his parents were constantly on the move. He
had already been round the world three times visiting
most of the countries en route and accumulating a
knowledge and interest of ships and navigation in the
early days of steam. His first voyage was in 1889,
when he went to New York in the *Adriatic*, a full-
rigged four-masted ship equipped with steam
engines. From New York he crossed America by the
Canadian Pacific Railway in an observation carriage
and then sailed from San Francisco to Japan.

His second voyage took him round the Horn in the
Kaikouro, a ship belonging to the New Zealand
Shipping Company. She carried tri-sails on her three
masts and was faster than the old *Adriatic*. The
weather, as usual, was bad when they rounded the
Horn but Dambom said he was far more worried by a
gang of young Australians who ran wild all over the
ship and I imagine, bullied the well-mannered little
English boy travelling with his parents. They called
at Australia and then sailed to New Zealand where
they stayed for some months visiting many of the
South Sea Islands in small local fishing boats.

On his third voyage my father visited Mexico and saw the heaps of rotting machinery which had been abandoned by Lesseps after his first attempt to build the Panama Canal when the killer 'yellow jack' claimed 20,000 men and over £50,000,000 was wasted on the ill-fated enterprise.

From Mexico he sailed to Honolulu and on to Japan for a second time.

When the young traveller was orphaned in his eighteenth year his guardian realized that his education had been gravely neglected and apart from a knowledge of geography and the fauna and flora of the various countries he had visited on his three global voyages, he knew none of the usual subjects necessary before going up to University. This lapse in his education was remedied after a year of serious study as a parlour boarder at Abingdon Grammar School after which he passed the necessary examinations to enter Brasenose College, Oxford.

While he was up at Oxford he spent several vacations sailing with his solicitor who taught him a great deal about navigation and cruising and this inspired him, in 1900, to buy his first cruising yacht, the *Bessy*, a small five-ton cutter. He sailed her, with great joy, until part of her keel fell off in Yarmouth Harbour and after that with less joy, when, although he thought half a keel was probably quite adequate, it certainly made sailing more hazardous, as there was a great art in being able to steer and manoeuvre her in a small estuary on a falling tide. Finally she fouled a very smart yacht belonging to a member of the Royal Yacht Squadron, knocking half the 'gingerbread' (gold filigree) off her bow and he decided to part with her.

After this experience he bought the thirteen-ton *Charm* and sailed her to Holland but after taking local advice - a thing he never did again - he grounded on a bank off Brille by the Hook of Holland. Although there was no sea, she bumped her keel off and fell right over, filling up with water and in a very short time was a total wreck. The timbers under her copper coating were so rotten they were useless even as firewood.

His next yacht was the nine-ton yawl, *Rothion*, in which he cruised for a number of years. In 1902, inspired by Erskine Childer's fascinating story *The Riddle of the Sands*, he sailed her to Holland with Scrase Saxby and on to the East Frisian Islands of Borkum, Norderney and Wangerooge before continuing on his way to the Hardanger Fjord on the west coast of Norway.

In 1910 he sailed her up to Skye and laid her up that autumn in a yard on the Crinan canal. The following year he married Scrase's sister Irene Saxby, and took his bride up to Scotland for a two months' honeymoon sailing *Rothion* in the Western Isles.

My mother never really enjoyed sailing and suffered constantly from seasickness but she adapted herself to life on board and was a most reliable mate, helmsman and cook, undertaking whatever was required of her in a most courageous manner.

1899 – *Gossip*

Gossip is a thirteen-ton cutter with a ten-foot beam
a draught of six feet, and thirty feet on the water-line.
She has considerable sheer forward and a counter
stern. Her topsides are of teak with pitchpine under
water and her mast is of spruce. She is gaff-rigged
with a roller jib and a foresail sheeted on to a horse
and is at her best with topsail set and a fresh wind on
the beam.

She was designed and built by Harris at Rowhedge
near Colchester in 1899 for Mr. E. Whitehead, who
sailed her for eight years, based on the east coast,
before selling her to Mr. E. W. Harrison and his
partner Mr. F. J. Rynd. Little is known of her
movements at that time except that she moved to the
south coast with her new owners who sold her in
1913 to Mr. John Rew. He owned her through the
war years and in 1919 she came to the Isle of Wight
with her fourth owner, Mr. Bruce Atkey.

Mr. Atkey, owner of the famous yacht chandlers in
Cowes High Street, was an expert in re-designing
yachts. He ranks high in my estimation as he altered
Gossip's steering gear from a tiller to a wheel, thus

making it possible for a child to handle her. Steering by tiller in a largish yacht is unsuitable for small children. It requires much more strength than a wheel and is tiring over long periods, especially in heavy weather. He also fitted the roller reefing gear which was efficient and easy to handle.

Mr. Atkey only owned *Gossip* for a year, but she was in excellent condition both above and below decks when he sold her in May 1920. At that time Dambom was looking for a yacht rather bigger than *Rothion* in which to cruise with his young and growing family.

Gossip and Dambom first became acquainted a few weeks later. She was lying on the slip at the Berthon boatyard in the Lymington River, and being right out of the water he could observe her lovely lines and fell in love with her at first sight. As he was gazing at her he heard a slow drawling voice across the yard, 'That's the boat for you. You buy 'er, Sir, she's modern.' And there was Tom Kelloway, pipe in mouth as usual, surveying man and boat together and realizing that they belonged to each other.

The contract was signed, the ship's papers handed over, and the following day Dambom, as the proud new owner, sailed her over to Yarmouth.

Bess and I stood excitedly on the Toll Bridge as she came up the harbour, then climbed the rails to get a better view. As soon as she was securely moored Dambom came to the jetty of the old sand house to fetch us, and Nanny, who had been Dambom's nanny before, handed us over with relief We went on board and drank tea out of porridge bowls and ate hunks of cheese which seemed to be the only food on board, but it made a welcome change from our nursery fare of milk and bread and jam. We were into everything, exploring every nook and cranny, burrowing through the sail lockers at the end of the bunks in the after cabin and emerging triumphantly on deck by the steering wheel.

Bess was seven at this time, very like Dambom, dark, thin, active and practical. As she was the first born it was only natural that she was christened 'Bess'. My father called all his first things by this name. It was the name of his mother and of the great aunt with whom he used to live, and in quick succession came his first yacht, his horse 'Black Bess', his dog and his first child, all bearers of the same name.

I was eighteen months younger, born three months before the First World War. I was christened Cecily after my father, but was so unlike the others with my red curly hair and freckles and love of books and poetry that I seriously thought I was a changeling and always lived a little outside life in a hidden world of make-believe.

Lucia, the third daughter, was born the year we bought *Gossip* and scarcely counted in the early days when Bess and I served our apprenticeship.

By the time Alan was born in 1926 we were all three members of the crew and Dambom had already evolved his theme, 'The girls and I can manage.'

Apart from removing a small stove used for heating purposes in the saloon and re-covering the settees himself, Dambom made very few alterations to *Gossip*'s interior.

The saloon, which was reached by a sharp descent of the companion steps, was a really comfortable and spacious room with settees on either side which formed sleeping berths at night. The folding table between the seats was fixed to the floor but when it was unbolted it swung with the motion of the ship and balanced its contents even in the roughest seas. The room was lined with mahogany panelling and the doors, locker tops and cupboards were all made of the same rich, well-polished wood. Oil looking-lamps fitted into brass sconces stood above the centre of each seat and the clock and barometer were fixed to the forward bulkhead. As in all well-designed yachts every available space was utilized. There were sufficient lockers, cupboards and shelves to store all the food, clothes, books and charts essential for a long cruise.

The saloon opened into the after-cabin which contained two good bunks with the 'loo' between them, over which was a large and heavy drawer which pulled out and turned into a wash-basin supplied by its own water tank. Lockers and drawers, made of mahogany as in the saloon, were fitted below the bunks and a ship's candle, fitted into a swinging sconce, gave a faint flickering light to the occupant of each bunk.

For'ard of the saloon was the fo'c's'le or galley with one cot bunk which folded up against the ship's side when not in use. Almost everything which hadn't a home anywhere else lived in the fo'c's'le, but it all tucked away under the seats with the paraffin, or in the forepeak - a regular glory hole - or even under the floorboards with the anchor chain. A huge spare Nicholson anchor was lashed to the foot of the mast which made manoeuvring in the small doorway a great feat when carrying plates of food from the galley to the saloon.

Cooking arrangements consisted of a double burner Rippingale stove with an oven, and a blue-flame stove wired to the floor which was quick and efficient provided that the wick was constantly cleaned and there wasn't too much draught from the fore-hatch, which was directly above.

Thomas also lived in the fo'c's'le. He deserves a special mention as he became such a favourite that we had him as our mascot and the symbol on our racing flag. Thomas was our bucket - blue on a yellow background for the flag. He was really christened by my father in a mistaken belief that it was Sir Thomas Moore (and not Sir John) who was buried 'at dead of night'. It is a rule in various ports, especially in Denmark, that no refuse may be tipped into the harbour. This proves to be a great problem for yachtsmen whose gash buckets are filled to bursting and so the natural, if undesirable, outcome was that 'Thomas' was discharged at dead of night.

Thomas had a near relation, 'Cousin Thomas', who lived on deck and was made of canvas and used for swilling decks. Latterly there were more relations including 'Yellow Thomas' who was made of plastic, and a useful invention of strong paper bags - known officially as 'Garbina' - became 'Paper Thomas'. When these ran out there was a poor relation known as 'Poor Man's Paper Thomas' which was just any old bag strong enough to hold a measure of garbage.

Also in the fo'c's'le we carried a vast prawning net inscribed 'Gravelines' which came out when conditions were favourable, but was used as a clothes line for towels and bathing things for most of its life.

Gossip boasted no depth finders or other modern navigational instruments and only carried a Hughes compass for steering and a telltale compass in the saloon. Sounding was done with a lead-line and distance covered recorded by a log-line which was trailed astern when making long passages.

Life-jackets were carried in the sail-locker. They were of the old and probably original style, very bulky canvas objects filled with cork. Bess and I tried them on one day under Dambom's guidance and looked so like Tweedledum and Tweedledee that we really went into battle and found them great fun as we could punch each other with great ferocity and remain unhurt although we tumbled and bounced about the deck like rubber dolls. We called them our 'body builders' and often put them on for fun but never sailed in them as they were so restricting that once tied into them we were severely hampered and so clumsy about the decks that we became a natural hazard not only to ourselves but to everybody else.

1920-26 – Early Days

When Lucia was a year old and a governess known as 'Dicky' had been persuaded to replace Nanny and look after the three of us, my parents made their first cruise in *Gossip*. They sailed across the Channel to Calais and were pleased with her performance in a heavy sea. From Calais they sailed to Gravelines and had to tack up the narrow canal for two miles before they reached the basin. This was a great test of her windward powers and she passed with flying colours.

From Gravelines, where they bought the great prawning net, they hired a car and toured the battlefields of the Somme and my mother had a terrible experience when she sank almost to her waist in the treacherous mud near Nieuwpoort.

The following year Bess had her first trip and after that we went in turns for a week or two at a time.

Dambom was a gentle master. He seldom shouted or swore at us, which is why we are still happy to crew for him after fifty years together. Friends of ours, also girls, who started sailing at the same time, were so ruled and disciplined by their father, that as soon as they were old enough to fend for themselves they vowed never to sail with him again and, in fact, grew up with a loathing of the sea. Obedience is essential on a yacht, especially when small children form part of the crew, and every command must be carried out immediately. Bess and I realized this but we knew we could ask questions afterwards and gradually we understood the rudiments of sailing until the orders appeared to be just common sense and a pattern of life developed in which we could see the move ahead as we all three thought on the same lines. The term 'a happy ship' has become rather hackneyed but it certainly applied to *Gossip*. Sailing with Dambom made for a life full of surprises but with him as skipper we always enjoyed ourselves.

I went on my first cruise when I was eight years old. I slept in the fo'c's'le with the fore-hatch open so that I could look out of my bunk and see the stars overhead. This made me curious about them so I quickly learnt the names of the main constellations and the first magnitude stars, and one glorious night I saw the whole of the Great Bear framed in the hatchway directly over my head. There was also a tiny porthole through which I could peep, but the most perfect thing was to lie quite still and listen to the sea creaming under the fore-foot. There is no sound quite like this. It is at its best in a river anchorage when the tide is running hard. Sometimes during the bad days of the war when the bombs were falling all round me, I would try and shut my ears to the noise and imagine that I was lying in my bunk listening to the whispered gossip of the waves as they hurried past the ship's sides on their way to the open sea. I would imagine I could hear the call of the oyster-catchers as they moved to new sandbanks at low water and the thrilling, rippling, bubbling notes of the curlews in the early morning as I had heard them so often in the Newtown River.

I soon learnt to make myself useful on deck and haul up the peak halyard with great gusto while my father took the heavier throat halyard to hoist the mainsail. I learnt to steer by the feel of the wind on my cheek and by watching the sails for the slightest flutter when I was keeping her close to the wind. I loved sitting in the commanding position astride the wheel-locker controlling the ship. I used to compare *Gossip* to a horse with a tender mouth and try to steer her gently by feel, without forcing the wheel, but sometimes in strong winds she became a different being and took the bit between her teeth and then I had to use a hand of iron to control her. She was a lovely boat to steer and I was never so happy as when I was at the wheel. I could steer for hours on end and never tire of it. Once I did a seven-hour stretch, no one else really cared for it, especially when it meant an accurate course on the compass, and years later when I sailed alone with my father it was a great asset as he preferred the active work and the navigation and liked to leave the steering to me.

I suffered a great deal from seasickness. In the early days it was a 'hit or miss' affair and there were often calls for 'Cousin Thomas' to swill the decks but I soon learnt to reach the lee rail and although I longed to lay my head on even the hardest of deck cushions, I realized early in life that once down it was difficult to rise again and so I grabbed my faithful wheel and forced myself to concentrate on the course. I became so adept at this, or so I thought, that I hardly lost my bearings in my quick darts to the rail but years later I was shattered when I was steering an Admiral's yacht and after two or three seconds over the side I returned with my usual promptness to be told that I was 'five degrees off course'. I had taken a little longer than usual because it was after I had knocked out my front tooth on the telephone and before vomiting I had to remove my 'territorials' (irregulars) and then replace them before my witch-like gap was noticed.

In the early days before *Gossip* had an engine, we were often left for hours just short of our destination waiting for a breath of wind or a fair tide. Sometimes my father would get out one of the huge sweeps and supporting it in what we called the 'giant's rowlock' would stand facing the bow pushing the great oar through the water. An alternative to this was to tow *Gossip* from the dinghy, which he would row with strong steady strokes, making surprisingly good progress. On one occasion he was sailing with my mother and his cousin Id. They spent a day idling along the coast from Swanage, hoping to make the peaceful little anchorage of Worbarrow Bay before sunset, but the light wind faded away and all hope of reaching the anchorage was dying. My father had fallen down the fore-hatch two days before and broken two of his ribs which were strapped firmly to his side so that he was unable to row. This left my mother and Id, so there was nothing for it but to put them to the sweeps. Dambom described them to me as he remembered them, sitting side by side on the fore-hatch, their long skirts spread out, their sleeves rolled up and their stockinged feet in white tennis shoes pressed firmly against the horse of the staysail. They had some difficulty in lifting the heavy sweeps and soon my father was crying out with pain as he laughed at their efforts and prayed to them to stop. This goaded them to further activity and they soon found the metre of the strokes and with fierce determination succeeded in rowing the thirteen-ton yacht into the anchorage.

My father suffered worst, or thought he did, as his painful ribs had to be re-bandaged with strips of sailcloth to repair the damage done by so much laughing and the blistered hands and the aching backs of the two women passed unnoticed.

Uncle Judy was a regular crew at this time. Although he was my godfather, I never knew his proper name. He had been my father's great friend at Oxford and as Dambom rejoiced in the name of

Punch, due to his somewhat hooked nose, his friend had automatically been labelled Judy. One August when he was crewing for my parents, they sailed west from Yarmouth and after a leisurely week of light easterly airs anchored for the night in a pleasant reach of the River Dart. The following morning they decided to call on Great Aunt Ada who was married to the rector of Totnes. They started off at seven in the morning in a flat calm and a fair tide and a very early edition of the now popular outboard motor fixed to the dinghy. It was not only the earliest but certainly the most unsuccessful. It was an absolute brute to start and couldn't even keep going when my father eventually got a kick out of it, so he abandoned it at Dittisham and then took to the oars with my mother to help him as Uncle Judy developed a headache and rested in the stern. They had a well-earned picnic lunch at Totnes and then went ashore to visit Great Aunt Ada. Alas, she was indisposed and when they introduced themselves to Uncle Charles, the rector, who had been summoned from his study, he said, 'I am so sorry, you must forgive me but I don't think I know you. I meet so many people.'

He did offer them some indifferent sherry, after which they returned to the dinghy and rowed eight miles back to the anchorage where they arrived in a state of exhaustion at seven in the eve. So much for Great Aunt Ada.

After this experience my father decided to fit an engine in *Gossip*, and before the next summer she was equipped with a little 6h.p. Day motor which could drive her at a modest three and a half knots in a calm but proved invaluable in harbours and rivers and was an asset when going to windward.

During these probationary years we went on a variety of short cruises mostly to the west, sailing sometimes as far as Fowey. They followed very much the same pattern and the highlights which seem to stand out in my mind were such things as the annual visit to the theatre in Weymouth, where I first saw 'The Mikado', the donkey rides on the beach and the great excitement of rounding Portland Bill where the tide runs at eight knots during springs and the seas are always frightening and the rocks, which have to be hugged to avoid the Race, menacing and forbidding. I remember the pleasant things ashore, such as looking for wild flowers which my father could always identify and searching the lovely pools at Worbarrow for sea anemones and sea hares, or squatting motionless on the rocks listening to the faint delicate scratching noise of limpets munching.

Dambom, brought up with little or no education in his early youth, thought it only mildly necessary for his daughters and had no compunction in calling us from our lessons if he wanted anything done on the yacht. We were only too pleased with this arrangement. One of our special treats was washing *Gossip*'s mainsail.

At the end of every season the sails were taken ashore and stored in the old coach house. The jibs, foresail and topsail were soaked in a large hip-bath in the stable yard and dried out on the stones, but washing the mainsail was quite another matter and only took place every second year. The heavy sail, still bound up with tyers, was brought up from the stable in a wheelbarrow and dumped like a huge anaemic sausage in the middle of the croquet lawn. We then untied the fastenings and spread the whole 280 square feet of canvas over the grass. Dambom would then connect the garden hose and play the water over the sail until it was all thoroughly soaked. As soon as the surplus water had run off, he would test to see if all the salt had been washed out by licking a bit of the canvas, much as a wine taster samples a vintage wine. When he was satisfied with the tasting the real work of the day would begin.

Bess and I, with bare feet and our cotton dresses tucked into our knickers, would each be given a cake of yellow soap and a hard scrubbing brush. Starting at the peak, we would scrub our way over the entire length and breadth of the sail while Dambom kept up a steady flow of water from the hose and followed us with a third scrubber to remove all traces of soap. He always chose a good long sunny day for this job and after our labours the sail was left on the lawn until the sun dried and bleached the canvas to a dazzling whiteness.

It was only years afterwards that we were told by a sailmaker that flax canvas sails, such as *Gossip*'s, should never be washed with soap.

Meanwhile Bess and I were learning to sail in home waters in the best way of all, in a boat of our own with a cut-down oar for a mast and a sail modelled from an old bath towel. We had just moved from Great Aunt Bessy's house in Freshwater to our late cousin's house, Norlands, which overlooked Yarmouth harbour and was so close to the sea that we had only to climb over the wall at the bottom of the garden, run across the road and we were in the little secret copse which hid the Admiral's steps and led straight down to the creek.

The boat, called *Euphrosyne*, was hardly one of the Graces. She had been used for many years by Jim Young, an old retainer who disliked walking so every morning if the tide served he would row the old boat over from Yarmouth and come right up the creek to the Admiral's steps where he would moor her and then potter up the road to the house. After cleaning the shoes and doing a few small jobs he would shuffle off to catch the tide down the creek to the harbour. When the tide didn't serve he took the morning off. This happened very often as the creek dried out completely at low water and was unnavigable even for the flattest punt. Jim only survived our advent at Norlands by a few months and it was then that Bess and I became the proud possessors of a boat.

A first boat is always exciting and even though *Euphrosyne* was a rough clinker-built dinghy painted a dark grey and certainly not in her prime, we adored her. We took her right up the Yar River exploring every inlet and creek, sailing with our jury-rig whenever possible and rowing the rest of the time or sculling over the stern. We certainly learnt about tides the hard way, and were often to be seen wading in the soft river mud towing poor old *Euphrosyne* behind us.

The Admiral's steps, where *Euphrosyne* lived, were made in 1781 for my great-great-grandfather. They still belong to us today although they are covered with mud and brambles and the council have designs on the secret wood as a suitable site for lavatories for the crowds of people who swarm all over the sand-spit. In 1847 Dambom's grandfather, the Admiral's son, was killed in action at sea while serving in the Royal Navy in command of a frigate. He had previously requested that in the event of his death his corpse should be taken up the creek to the Admiral's steps and conveyed from there to Freshwater Church. However, when the time came the Naval Officer conducting the funeral took one look at the creek and said he couldn't risk his gig in such a place. Finally great-grandfather was carried from his ship in the Yarmouth Roads in the Admiral's gig, rowed three miles up the Yar to the causeway, which lies just below the church and laid to rest in the family vault in Freshwater churchyard. The gig was kept by the family and when we came to live at Norlands it was set upright beside the croquet lawn making a favourite seat for the onlookers and a romantic hideout for his great-grandchildren.

In June, 1925, Dambom, with two friends, sailed *Gossip* out to Denmark and laid her up in a little private boatyard at Svendborg, on the island of Fyn, owned by Tibbie Weber, the famous yacht designer. Strangely enough, in this same small yard he found the yacht *Patience*, also from the Isle of Wight, belonging to Tom Perrot of the Royal Cruising Club.

Dambom had hoped to take *Gossip* on to Norway the following year, but his fourth child was due that autumn, so he decided to leave the yacht in Denmark for another year. To console himself during this year of inactivity he sailed with Colonel J.F.N. Baxendale - his C.O. in the Hampshire Yeomanry - in his superb fifty-ton cutter *Hallowe'en*.

This queen of ships, measuring seventy feet overall, was entered for the Fastnet race that year and after some practice races in the Solent, Dambom signed on as one of the crew.

This was the second of the now famous Fastnets and the first to be sailed under the newly formed Ocean Racing Club which had come into being at the conclusion of the first race the previous year.

Nine yachts answered the gun fired from the Royal Yacht Squadron on August 14th, including the first American entry, the schooner *Primrose IV*.

They encountered a variety of conditions on this 600-mile race, including calms, sudden squalls, fog and finally a Force 8 gale.

Early on in the race, in a sudden increase of wind, Colonel Baxendale ordered his crew to reef the much criticized modern Bermudan mainsail. This proved a difficult task as there were no reefing-points and the sail had to be laced down with unused rope. This of course was soon in a thousand tangles and eventually had to be cut into short lengths.

Hallowe'en was the first round the Fastnet but Colonel Baxendale spent several minutes calling up the lighthouse-keeper with a flash lamp in order to ascertain this fact. Dambom, meanwhile, was asked to set a course, so thinking it was only a temporary measure while the skipper was otherwise engaged, he told the helmsman to steer on a reciprocal course.

Unfortunately this was never checked, and when Dambom came on watch again four hours later, he was horrified to find the yacht still on the same course.

When they sighted land Dambom realized it was Cape Cornwall, and then followed a two-hour slog to windward, which probably lost them the race, as it was only due to their inaccurate navigation that they were in that unhappy position.

Their troubles were not yet over. Just as they were abeam of Rame Head the main halyard parted and the mainsail descended of its own accord as the slides slipped off the track, leaving festoons of white canvas flapping all over the deck. The confusion was indescribable, it was as though a large marquee had collapsed on its inmates in a gale of wind. All hands struggled to free themselves before they were swept overboard by the unruly sail. It was some time before they had it under control, safely lashed to the boom and they continued the race tacking up the harbour to the finishing line at Drake's Island under headsails alone. Dambom described himself as a 'human cleat' at this stage as he had to hold the staysail to windward to help the yacht about every time she tacked.

Hallowe'en was first across the finishing line, but on corrected time the race was won by *Ilex*, owned by the Royal Engineers, with the American yacht *Primrose IV* second and *Hallowe'en* third.

Hallowe'en completed the course in 3 days, 19 hours and 5 minutes, a record that stood until 1965 when *Gitana IV*, owned by Baron de Rothschild, sailed the course in 3 days, 9 hours and 40 minutes. From 1925 until 1961 the race was sailed eastward from Cowes round the Isle of Wight, thus adding about thirty miles to the distance. After that time they started to westward and sailed through the Needles Channel.

Hallowe'en, now rigged as a yawl and renamed *Cotton Blossom*, still sails off the east coast of America. Her present owner has said he would like to enter her once again in the Fastnet race. I hope he will do so; it would be interesting to see how she compares with a modern ocean racer.

After this historic race Dambom became a member of the small exclusive Ocean Racing Club (O.R.C.) – exclusive because only those who had completed the Fastnet race were eligible for membership – so *Gossip* was entitled to fly the coveted burgee of the O.R.C., in 1931 to become the R.O.R.C., which has my favourite sea horse as its emblem.

1927 – Three Northern Capitals

In 1927 my father reckoned that Bess and I had served our apprenticeship and were ready to rank as able seamen. We had missed *Gossip* sadly during the last two years and though the advent of a baby brother the previous October had been some consolation, we couldn't wait to get on board again.

I was thirteen at the time and Bess a year older. It was our first trip abroad and our first proper cruise and the excitement was intense. With my father as skipper, my mother as mate and Bess and me as crew, we were a full ship's complement. We travelled out to Esbjerg in the *Empress of Scotland* wearing our new crew's uniform of navy-blue jerseys and pleated skirts, white shoes and socks and straw hats with navy-blue bands on which had been painted the gay red and white colours of the Royal Cruising Club burgee. From Esbjerg we continued our journey by train to Odense and Svendborg.

This was to be a serious cruise and our aim was to visit three Northern capitals, Copenhagen, Oslo and Stockholm, and submit our log to the Royal Cruising Club at the end of the season, when such journals are judged by the Commodore and various cups awarded for the best cruises.

We arrived at Svendborg during the afternoon of July 30th and soon we were on the sunny wharf at Hestehauge eagerly gazing down at *Gossip* with our baggage, in numerous sail-bags, piled around us. It couldn't have been hotter as we toiled away stowing blankets, mattresses, clothes and stores, and finally as a last straw, Bess and I filled the canvas water bags from the hand pump on the quay and carried them on board again, and again, and again, until we had thirty gallons of water in the two tanks. Work over we revived ourselves with a refreshing bathe and then rowed up the river to Christianmunde where we had a well-earned dinner in beautiful surroundings under the trees.

Next morning was spent rigging *Gossip* as Dambom always liked to do this himself. We hoisted him up in the bosun's chair and handed him rope after rope as he worked out the very complicated cat's cradle of the peak and throat halyards, the topsail sheets and jib and foresail halyards.

In the evening the Webers invited us to tea and plied us with little cakes and sandwiches. They showed us amongst their treasures a lamp-shade delicately fashioned by Hans Andersen depicting some of his little people.

On August 1st we were ready for sea and with sails set we waved goodbye to the friendly Webers. We made Lohals that first day, only about sixteen miles but it was good to have started and all went well.

We soon developed a routine on board and after a few days it seemed as though we had been at sea for weeks. Dambom was always first up in the morning and after rousing Bess and me who slept in the saloon he would entice us on deck for a swim. He

bathed every day, a quick splash as he dived in and
then a rattle and shake as he climbed the bobstay and
heaved himself back on board. We followed more
reluctantly and had some difficulty in climbing the
bobstay and working our bare feet along the wire
stays before we regained the safety of the deck. As
an alternative to bathing, Bess and I would
sometimes row ashore and get milk while breakfast
was being cooked. This was always fun in an
unknown country. We had to go early to the farms to
get the milk before it was separated.

Dambom always cooked breakfast. He put the
kettle on 'blueflame' before his bathe and by the
time he had dried himself on deck it would be
boiling. He would then make the porridge and put it
to bubble away on top of the slower Rippingale
stove. While the kettle was re-boiling for the coffee,
he would break eggs haphazardly into the pan,
adding tomatoes, potato remains, bacon, mushrooms
and anything edible found in the vicinity. When all
was cooking and the coffee made and keeping hot on
the Rippingale, he would call for one of the crew to
make toast while he repaired to the after cabin to
dress and shave with the remains of the hot water.

Toast making was an art in itself. It was made on
top of 'blueflame' and needed constant attention. At
its best it turned out well browned in the centre with
branded marks of the stove all round and a hard dry
white crust where the bread lay outside the area of
the flame. At its worst and more usual state, it was
blackened and flavoured with paraffin, or part white,
part black according to the mood of the crew, the
tempering of 'blue-flame's' wick and the strength of
the overhead draft from the fore-hatch which caused
the stove to smoke.

After breakfast we divided forces, one of us
working on deck with Dambom and the other doing
chores below decks with the mate. The deck hand
had to get the sails ready for setting and help
Dambom with the anchor. He knelt on the deck, with

his bare feet pressed firmly against a cleat, turning the capstan with a single handle. His crew had to heave the chain behind him and guide it down the deck hole to the fo'c's'le, where it invariably fouled the workers below decks who were by then washing up. It was sometimes a long and tedious job, especially when we anchored in some of the deep water fjords when fathom after fathom of cable would be hauled in on the hand capstan.

In spite of the hard work involved in retrieving the anchor and sometimes also the kedge, below decks was always considered the inferior job. It consisted of sweeping the carpets in both cabins, filling the oil looking-lamps and then sitting with the mate, one on either side of Thomas, washing up dinner and breakfast things in the minimum of water and stowing them away in the tiny pantry. It was done against time and also such adversities as the anchor chain, which was first ripped up, removing the floor-boards, as it was put round the capstan and then coiled in a wet pile at our feet from where it had to be stowed under the floor-boards once more.

We were usually underway at about nine o'clock and all were on deck by then ready to set the sails. Lunch was eaten on deck in fine weather and we aimed at reaching our anchorage by five or six o'clock in the evening so that we could explore ashore and have a walk before cooking dinner. This was the main meal of the day and usually cooked by the mate with one of the crew acting as assistant. We had some excellent roasts cooked in the little Rippingale oven with the vegetables simmering away on top and it was quite possible to cook underway as we often did if we were late reaching our anchorage.

After dinner we would light the oil lamps in the saloon which made it warm and cosy, and play a game of ludo or racing-demon and write our logs. Bedtime was disturbing, as each in turn we washed and undressed by a single swinging candle in the congested after cabin, then, collecting our pile of blankets, had to push our way through the narrow doorway, dropping things as we came. Beds had to be made and pillowcases found and pulled over the day cushions which always seemed a tedious job after a long day.

We reached Copenhagen, the first of our capitals, in three days and picked up a buoy in the large harbour where everyone waved to us in a most friendly manner. We spent the next day ashore sightseeing and dining at the Yacht Club.

From Copenhagen we sailed up the Sound to the Narrows, and as we glided past the beautiful castle of Elsinor I sat perched in the bow, glued to the binoculars, half hoping, half dreading to see the ghost of Hamlet's father with his 'sable silver'd beard', still lurking on the ramparts. The opposing flags were flying on either side of us. The red and white of Denmark to port and the blue and yellow of Sweden to starboard.

We had a fair wind up the Kattegat and set the spinnaker, making seventy-one miles in the day and tying up alongside a raft of logs in the evening, close to the port of Halmstad. We found a farm where we bought fresh butter and milk that evening and Bess and I were presented with a bag of cherries. After dinner we stood on the raft and had a competition to see how far we could spit our cherry stones until it became too dark to find our shot.

We continued our way to Oslo, averaging about forty miles a day, enjoying the intricate navigation between the islands. Food was often difficult to find in our anchorages and when we did come across a small 'handel' (village shop) the bread was apt to be full of carraway-seeds which we disliked intensely.

One lovely day we anchored for lunch in a tiny inlet and Bess and I swam ashore and found an uninhabited island covered with wild raspberries. We ate as many as we could before swimming back to *Gossip* for lunch. Another time we found bilberries which we picked and stewed for dinner.

We scarcely noticed the boundary between Norway and Sweden on our way north. Luckily the Norwegian buoyage is very similar to that of Sweden. They use spars, red or black, instead of the little red brushes or magpie perches favoured by the Swedes. In both countries the marking of the intricate passages is very good and clear.

In Norway we had our first 'smørgasbord'. This national institution consists of a large central table laden with about a hundred dishes. About half would be some type of sea food, including our favourite smoked salmon, some very good soused herrings and large succulent prawns. The meat dishes consisted of a variety of cold sausage meats and thin slices of smoked ham. In addition to these there would be egg dishes, salads and great slabs of dark brown goats' milk cheese (gjetost) which had to be cut in flakes so thin that they rolled up on the plate. Sometimes also a hot dish would be served from a huge casserole on the side table.

My parents, being diffident by nature, fared badly at these public feasts, but Bess and I, being entirely uninhibited, would walk back from the table again and again with loaded plates and glasses of milk.

Gossip continued on her way up the Oslo fjord with a good proportion of fair winds. We only set the spinnaker on light days when Dambom felt there was no risk of a sudden increase of wind. This was because with the big sail and very heavy spinnaker boom, manning the guy and sheet by hand in any weight of wind proved a great strain and if the wind freshened, the three of us would have had a hard tussle to get the sail down.

One day we set the balloon foresail as a spinnaker, jacking it out on a sweep but in a sudden squall the sweep snapped off at the blade and we had a difficult time retrieving the thin billowing sail.

We reached Oslo, the second of our capitals, on August 14th, just two weeks out from Svendborg and celebrated with a day ashore. We paid homage at the shrine of the Viking ship from Gokstad and took the electric train up the mountain to Froquersaetter, 1,400 feet above the fjord. We ate our lunch, which ended with the biggest mound of raspberries and ice cream I had ever seen, in the little log hut looking out on the fjord miles below.

The next day we started our return passage down the Oslo fjord. At the Norwegian-Swedish border this time a very officious Customs officer came alongside as we prepared to anchor and insisted that we should go on to Stromstad at once, although he came on board and made a preliminary search, consulting frequently with his mate in the launch. Eventually Dambom persuaded him that we were starving and he relented so far as to allow Bess and me to row ashore for provisions but took good care to see that we went empty-handed. The natives ashore were much more friendly and we succeeded in buying bread, butter and milk at a lonely farmstead and the farmer's wife gave us a present of salted prawns which we enjoyed for dinner.

Next morning we put in to Stromstad and a polite Customs official came on board and made a wonderful survey of the ship, not omitting to check through the mate's suitcase, to her intense indignation. He then proceeded to list our gear - 4 anchors, 45 fathoms of chain, ¼lb butter, 2 eggs - but here he began to wilt and abandoned the task - although we had to stay on board until the Commander-in-Chief arrived in his launch.

We had a rough passage down the coast to Göteborg. We put three rolls in the mainsail and rolled up the jib. Rain fell heavily and it was so miserable on deck that we took short spells at the wheel and then went below to warm up. We were thankful to anchor in Marstrand harbour that evening but not so happy later on when we realized that there was a yacht race from Göteborg in progress and the night was made hideous with the noise of the shouting men, the flapping of canvas sails and the rattling of anchor chains which kept us awake until the last yacht arrived at dawn.

On August 22nd we entered the Göta Canal, leaving the sea behind us, with nearly 200 miles to go across Sweden before we could reach the Baltic on the other side at Mem, 100 miles south of Stockholm.

Our first sight of the Göta River was exciting; the current was running fiercely against us and the wind blowing even more fiercely astern. We put in three reefs and charged the stream with considerable success. On either side of us were reeds and almost no habitation, when out of the blue came a Customs launch which ran alongside us while one of the occupants came on board and searched us once more, again with a complete lack of tact, having a 'go' at the mate's suitcase. We tied up alongside a derelict pier for the night and made a few changes in *Gossip*'s rig to make her less vulnerable in the canal. The main adjustment was to remove her bowsprit and ship it on the deck. In spite of these precautions we developed some nasty bruises and scars on our white hull during the next ten days, a disease which became known as the 'Göta rash'.

We met our first lock in the stormy Göta River. Then followed another river passage before we reached the great Trollhätten locks. These locks had been modernized and were all electrically controlled, four of them taking the place of the twelve rock-hewn variety which Dambom had taken *Rothion* through over twenty years before.

Next day we had a scare when we were waiting for a railway bridge to open. The stern warp parted with a snap and *Gossip* charged towards the bridge at an alarming rate. Luckily Bess let go the anchor just in time to bring her up, probably saving the mast.

Soon after this we reached Lake Vänern, the largest of the great string of lakes which make the map of Sweden look like an intricate piece of fretwork. The lake is so big (110 miles by 80 miles) that we imagined we were at sea again and were soon out of sight of land.

We spent the first night on this lake close to the shore in a little inlet where the pine trees came down to the water's edge. Fresh water is a scarce commodity on board when every drop has to be carried to the tanks in canvas bags, so we revelled in the clean, clear water of the lake and scooped it up in Cousin Thomas, filling the tanks, the kettle, the washing-up bowl and every available utensil. Having done all this Bess and I were sent ashore with a large cake of soap and a towel and given orders to wash ourselves and our hair before we returned to the ship.

It was fascinating sailing through the various lakes which were all linked by rivers or canals. Roxen is perhaps the most beautiful. Bess and I had a nerve-racking time there because Dambom fell on the deck and nearly knocked himself out just as we were going through the narrow rock-bound entrance. He retired below leaving us to steer and navigate through the intricate passage. Bess was quick and accurate reading the charts so I took the wheel and followed her instructions. Younger sisters are drilled to obedience early in life and on the whole we worked very well together. Certainly on this occasion we were successful and by the time Dambom had recovered we were clear of Lake Roxen and into the last stretch of the canal.

The little engine was invaluable for the canal work on its good days but it was decidedly erratic and when it failed, Bess and I would walk the tow-path yoked together, dragging *Gossip* with a steady 'two-girl' power. We quite enjoyed this but were often so engrossed in our conversation that we failed to notice hazards on the canal bank and Dambom had to shout to us to stop so that we could push the boat away from the hazard before continuing on our way.

The islands ashore were full of interesting wild life. On one occasion we discovered whole colonies of wood ants living in huge anthills made of pine

needles. Another time we found a profusion of
cranberries and filled the milk can with them after
ten minutes' picking. The mate lost no time in
converting them into delicious cranberry jam with
which we replenished our dwindling store cupboard.

The descent from the lakes to Mem was a very slow
business with bridges and locks at short intervals.

The locks were all of the old style and most of the
time we had to work them ourselves. Bess and I soon
mastered the technique. We found that by working
together we were just able to lift the heavy sluices
and after that, opening the lock gates was simple.
Shutting the sluices was another matter and Dambom
always undertook this after our first attempt when the
wheel got out of control and spun round so quickly
that we only just had time to jump clear of the
revolving spokes.

One day I saw a grass snake swimming round in
one of the locks and although we were churning
round in the bubbly water in our rapid descent to sea-
level at the time, I couldn't resist jumping into the
dinghy and capturing him. There was always plenty
to do when we were locking through, even if we
weren't actually working the sluices, so I just
dropped the slippery creature into the dinghy and
clambered back on board ready to take in the warp
before the lock-gates opened. My absence on deck
had barely been noticed, but I could hardly hide
Tiglath, as I named my new pet. Fortunately no one
objected to his presence in the dinghy as we didn't
need it for going ashore while we were in the canal
so for two days he settled down quite happily to boat
life. In the evenings I took him ashore and hoped he
would find his own food but he wasn't very
successful and he spurned the delicacies I offered
him. In the end Dambom persuaded me to release
him and so averted what might have been a tricky
situation when we wanted to use the dinghy again.

When we reached the last railway bridge, with
Mem in sight, we managed to get a rope round the

propeller. Exhausted, we left it until morning when Dambom spent two hours in the water moving the shaft and trying to unravel it. Success at last but the engine refused to start so Bess and I yoked ourselves together once more and towed our reluctant yacht to Mem.

It was good to be in the sea again, unrestricted and free, and poor bruised *Gossip* must have been pleased to lick her sores in the clean fresh water of the Baltic.

Four days later we reached our voyage's end and sailed into Stockholm harbour with its picturesque buildings and little wooded islands and white-sailed yachts of all sorts and sizes moving in every direction.

Bess and I were due back at school and had to leave with the mate the following day. Dambom waited for a friend to join him before returning to Göteborg where *Gossip* was laid up for the winter.

The cruise had taken us 900 miles through three strange countries. It had opened new gates for us and given us our first taste of the wanderlust. *Gossip* received her reward the following spring when Sir Arthur Underhill, the Commodore of the Royal Cruising Club, awarded Dambom the Romola Cup.

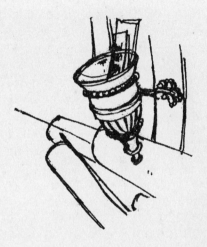

1928 – Norway: The Hardanger Fjord

A year is a very long time when you are fourteen years old, shut away in a boarding school for weeks on end, out of range of the curlews' call and out of sight of the sea. I found the summer term of 1929 especially long but eventually it dragged to a close, the dreary exams were over and I was home again discarding my hated black stockings and school uniform and packing my sailing clothes in my kitbag ready to join *Gossip* in far away Sweden.

For our cruise that year we planned to sail from Göteborg up the Kattegat and on to Strömstad on the Swedish coast; then across the Oslo fjord to Norway following the coast round the Naze and up northwards to the Hardanger fjord, which my father had visited in *Rothion* in 1903. We had Norwegian charts entitled 'special karts over den Norske Kyst' which we found very clear and easy to follow with the light sectors marked, and coloured track lines showing the best passages between the reefs and islands.

Dambom, the mate, Bess and I left Tilbury in the *Saga* and had a fair crossing of the North Sea. Early on the morning of July 30th we sailed up the Göta River past the shipyard where, to our dismay, we saw poor *Gossip*, mastless and forlorn, still on the slip. Luckily the owner of the yard came to meet us at Göteborg and explained - as he helped us through the Customs and packed us and our disreputable luggage into a taxi - that the incessant rain had delayed *Gossip*'s fitting out, but he promised to launch her within the hour.

At the wharf we made for the store and spread sails and bedding to air in the hot sun. Rats had made merry with the jib although fortunately that didn't matter as we had brought a spare but the leaks developed by the ship as soon as she took the water seemed very serious indeed. We were all very depressed and when the rain suddenly descended on us we packed all our gear under a tarpaulin and went out to lunch.

The owner recommended a little restaurant where we found a room to ourselves on the top floor overlooking the harbour, and we soon forgot the rain and the half-baked appearance of the boat as we absorbed the wonderful 'smørgasbord'. Not the least succulent dish was a local delicacy called the 'bird's nest', which consisted of hard boiled egg yokes surrounded by caviar.

Rain fell steadily all that afternoon and clad in oilskins and boots we shopped and stowed the gear. Bess and I were given the unenviable task of scrubbing the bottom boards with thick yellow soap and cold water, while Dambom cleaned out the water tank with his bath sponge and the mate sorted the stores and linen.

Next morning the effects of lunch had worn off and we spent a miserable day. Certainly the ship was leaking less seriously and pumping, though still the order of the day, was less strenuous. The welcome suction noise came after forty strokes when Bess and

I worked alternate 'tens' after breakfast. We still had all the floorboards up awaiting the arrival of the ballast and the desks were leaking badly. When we emerged from the squalor below decks we were greeted by icy rain. Dambom realized that another good luncheon was essential to keep up our morale so once again we repaired to our cosy restaurant and fortified ourselves for the work in hand. This was a strategic move because when we returned to the ship we found the ballast still in store. Dambom whipped up a gang to bring it on deck and lower it into the bilges by way of the peak halyard but they jibbed at the rain and soon cleared off leaving us to pass down the bulk of it ourselves. It was as well that we had been brought up in a hard school as this was certainly a test of our strength and endurance. Handling and shifting half-hundredweight pigs of lead and stowing them in their exact places in the bilges is no dainty job and I have seldom been given a more distasteful task. After two hours' work when all was complete, I proudly held out my oily, mutilated hands and surveyed the tom nails and bruised and bleeding fingers. 'You can always tell a lady by her hands,' I said, quoting a favourite theme of my governess.

'Sherlock Holmes would have no difficulty in determining our occupation', said Bess adding her mauled members for general inspection, 'Navvies or "off course" Amazons'.

Next day the sun shone. We rigged the ship and bent on the mainsail and the new jib so that by evening *Gossip* looked like a yacht once more. We then tried out the engine, motoring up stream towards the city. It ran very smoothly with its new main bearing which was a great relief after last year's performance.

'August 2nd: Bar reading 29.87. Wind N.W. light. Fine and bright.' Thus read the log and all augured well for our start. We were away at last on the swift Göta River, with no regrets at leaving the depressing yard. We had a good run to Marstrand but as we

cleared the narrows by Varholm to cross the Nord
Elf, a great thunderstorm full of wind and rain raged
overhead while Dambom and Bess rolled in three
reefs in the mainsail. It passed as suddenly as it had
come and the strength went out of the wind as we
anchored in the harbour and took a line astern to the
quay.

Marstrand was famous in our eyes for the high
quality of the dinner ashore where a hot dish was
always produced in addition to the excellent
'Smørgasbord', and also for the 'badhus' across the
harbour at Koon where there was a splendid water-
chute much patronized by Bess and me. We spent all
our spare time climbing the steps and then whizzing
down into the murky water of the harbour. I have
never done this anywhere else or even seen a similar
chute and we found it exhilarating and exciting. It
was excellent value at ten öre a time and before we
sailed next morning Bess and I begged for just one
more glorious plunge. Unfortunately this time
disaster hit me. Bess went first and I followed at a
safe distance but imagine my horror when I found I
had shot right into the middle of a shoal of
malevolent mahogany-coloured jelly-fish. Bess was
just clear of them but I was surrounded and their
horrible tentacles stretched out to molest me like the
arms of an angry octopus. I suppose I must have
given them a fright but they certainly had their
revenge. My arms and legs were badly attacked and
soon came out in a painful rash which worried me for
days, stinging like a thousand bee stings, burning in
the sun and irritating through the hot nights.

From Marstrand we made a steady progress up the
Swedish coast re-visiting Rafto and the surrounding
islands where we collected cranberries and bilberries.

We crossed the Oslo fjord sailing between
Torbjörnskjer and Grisbadarne Islands on a quiet
misty day steering on a compass course to keep clear
of the rocks. The wind headed us as we reached the
Norwegian coast and we had to make short tacks to

clear the Svenoer Islands. As we entered the natural harbour of Fredriksvaern the setting sun blazed crimson and purple above the outlying islands.

The fiery sunset produced a perfect day. When Dambom went on deck in the morning he was all for pressing on but he spotted a British yacht anchored nearby. After breakfast the owner, Mr. Lester Smythe, and his wife rowed across to us in their Norwegian 'yolla' (dinghy) and invited us to come ashore with them. They showed us the old church and the graves of English and German sailors whose bodies had been washed ashore. They then took us to a rope factory in a shed about 800 yards long where warps were being made for whalers. We watched the men making harpoon-gun lines which consisted of coils of Italian hemp, about four inches in diameter, attached to 500 fathoms of six-inch manilla. The old men walked backwards down the long room spinning the yam from bundles of hemp attached to their waists.

After lunch we invited the Smythes on board for coffee and they told us how some of Nelson's ships had been lured to their destruction on the Rakkebone, a large reef off the harbour entrance, by following the Norwegians who knew the channel.

A nice old 'Told' (Customs) officer came on board that afternoon and asked for a list of our stores implying in a most casual manner that anything would do. After Dambom had signed the paper he sealed it in an envelope with a great seal and said it would clear us in the future. It never did. The envelope was always taken ashore and brought back again with a local 'Told' stamp.

After this pleasant idle day we made an early start and were away by seven o'clock next morning. We had a lively beat when we emerged from the shelter of the islands but luckily it was short lived and we all weathered it. We anchored that evening in a great rock-bound pool near the island of Riso. It was here that we were visited by the kraken.

We had just returned from a ramble ashore laden with wild raspberries from Riso. Bess and I were busy in the fo'c's'le helping the mate convert them into jam while Dambom read his thriller in the saloon, when suddenly a mighty thud on the deck shook the ship and sent us all scurrying up the hatch in apprehensive excitement. As we emerged there was a great splash and a shower of spray but nothing to be seen either on board or in the sea. Bess and I searched the deck for any clue to the mystery but all we found was a large wet patch on the fore-deck which certainly hadn't been there when we returned from the island. Bess and my parents discussed the strange phenomenon for some time. Could it have been a dolphin? Or a porpoise? Or even a seal? I kept quiet, realizing that the others would only laugh at me, because I knew what it was. I knew it was a kraken.

I had read about this fabulous sea-monster at school. It was said to be capable of leaping on board a small fishing boat and crushing the ribs of a man in its iron grasp, before returning with him to the rocky caves at the bottom of the sea. It was described as a giant black squid of enormous strength and fearful appearance, which was sometimes seen off the Norwegian coast. I was too frightened to go on deck again that evening, yet secretly I longed to see it. I sat for some time in the fo'c's'le peeping out of the little porthole, but it never came back.

The next three days were slow and strenuous. *Gossip* had to fight head winds all the way. It was as though the kraken was holding us back. Sometimes I wondered if he was following the ship, biding his time before he selected his victim. On one occasion we left our anchorage heavily reefed and were greeted by the fishing boats coming back with their diminutive sails close reefed. After two hours outside we realized the misery and futility of pounding to windward in the murky turbulent seas and returned to our sheltered haven amongst the timber yards.

On August 11th, with the wind still in our teeth, we passed Kristiansand and were on our way between the small rocky islands. The navigation was intricate but we didn't fail to see the unusual portent in the sky when at one o'clock the sun was ringed by a complete vivid rainbow. Dambom, who was a very good weather prophet and relied on his observations of cloud formations, sunsets and sunrises etc. to help in his forecasting, thought this a very bad omen, foretelling unusually bad weather. As we were due to round the Naze of Norway the following day when fine weather with only a light wind was essential, he asked the 'Told' officer who came for our sealed envelope that evening for the local forecast. He reported fair weather and a south-east wind which seemed ideal for the course.

The man was right. Dambom called us early the following morning and after breakfast we made a good stow of all the gear below, ready for the heavy seas we expected to meet around the point. A really fair wind at last and Bess was sent tunnelling into the sail locker for the balloon foresail which she and Dambom set as a spinnaker. We rounded the Naze of Norway under this rig in a spanking breeze with the surf rolling and racing around us. This was one of the highlights of the cruise for me. Frightening, as all these races are. Spectacular, with the great masses of granite rocks towering above us and falling down to the breakers off the point, reminiscent of Portland Bill. I was lucky enough to be steering at the time. I thought Dambom would take the wheel from me when *Gossip* was whirled about in the bubbling maelstrom, but he must have sensed my excitement and the firm set of my jaw for he let me continue. I was exhilarated, terrified and determined. I wouldn't let go, and above all, I wouldn't look back. That was far too frightening. *Gossip* was a thoroughbred horse and I held the reins. I must be the master. She came through at last on a wild irregular course then surged ahead clear of the race. We all relaxed and chatted easily again, sucking some rather unpleasant sweets and thinking about lunch, long overdue.

The wind freshened in the afternoon. We took in the balloon foresail and reefed the mainsail. The glass fell two-tenths and dense rain squalls obscured the land and drenched us in the cockpit. An hour later we rolled in three more reefs and the gale hit us. It came up from astern with a sudden roar, sweeping *Gossip* along the crest of the waves. Dambom and Bess rolled in two more reefs, making seven in all, and bringing the claw of the gaff to within two feet of the boom. The sea, rough and gurly, thundered up the rocks in spite of the shelter of the high cliffs as we neared Rekefjord. How thankful we were that the Naze was behind us. It was a wild and stirring scene. White waterfalls cascaded down from the black cliffs which rose three or four hundred feet above the foam-flecked sea. We nosed in between the rocks beating through the narrows with just the jib and tiny peak of mainsail. Luckily the engine stood by us and helped us going about on each tack. As we sailed up to the lighthouse at the entrance to the fjord, a sudden gust of wind laid sturdy old *Gossip* on her side as if she had been a six-metre. I was relieved when we picked up a buoy at the end of the fjord. As the wind howled and funnelled up the valley between the mountains, Dambom recollected the solar rainbow of yester-eve...

Even in the land of midnight sun it seemed dark that evening. Black clouds hung over the fjord and cast a dark stain on the water. As soon as we had stowed the sails we all came below and shut down the hatches and skylights. We lit the looking-lamps in the saloon and heated up some mulligatawny soup on 'blueflame'. While the storm raged all round us we stayed below decks warm and cosy, enjoying our dinner with a feeling of exhilaration after our battle with the elements.

After the stormiest night Dambom ever remembered, we awoke to a peaceful morning and were able to appreciate the beauty of our land-locked anchorage. The barometer had already risen, but rather too quickly for Dambom's liking. He always mistrusted a sudden rise after a gale, considering it a warning of further bad weather to come. Bess and I searched both sides of the fjord for milk and came back triumphant with a full can and a bailer alive with fresh mackerel.

The Naze was behind us, but we still had Jaederens-Rev to face. A point of ill repute. At our first attempt the lumbering swell Of the North Sea was so forbidding that we turned tail. A day later, with a strong fair wind we tried again. With reefed mainsail we cleared the fjord and caught the full sea. It was so big that the boom dipped in the waves and we had to 'top' it up. A cloudburst knocked some of the kick out of the sea but when we rounded the point it slopped up on our quarter and surged over the decks. The dinghy, on thirty fathoms of warp, was surf-riding and then disappearing in the abyss of the waves. We looked astern dreading its sudden arrival on deck but it missed us each time. We anchored in Tananger Bay that night close to a large German yacht. We were only four miles from Stavanger, the centre of the sardine fishing fleet, but all was quiet in the Bay and we provisioned the ship at the one tiny 'handel' ashore.

Rounding Jaederens-Rev. (From left to right): Bess, Steering – Irene
Brent-Good (mother 'The Mate'), Cecily

Our engine refused to start next morning so we
made rather an ungraceful exit from our narrow berth
pushing off from a fish warehouse with the boat-
hook and aided by one of the Germans towing from
his dinghy. As we sailed clear he remarked: 'You
have a large piece of blotting-paper (seaweed) on
your anchor!'

Another day of rain and squalls, thunder and
lightning and no engine! However we moored
alongside a pier at a small village in the afternoon
and telephoned for a mechanic. He arrived within the
hour, examined our engine and found it full of salt
water which must have forced its way down the
exhaust pipe in the big seas off Jaederens-Rev. An
hour's work and a fee of five kroner (fifty pence)
repaired the damage.

We spent another four days sailing northwards,
sheltered from the North Sea by the range of islands.

We explored many beautiful fjords and every evening found us in a new and wonderful anchorage with unknown lands to visit ashore where we climbed and berry-hunted before returning to the ship to prepare dinner.

It was on the evening of the fourth day, after rounding the sheer iceberg-like island of Skorpen that we came to our Shangri-la, the dream hamlet of Sundal, lying at the foot of the Bondhusbrae glacier. A sprinkling of houses, a tiny pier and far, far above the great white plain of the Folgëfonni - the field of snow - which stretches for seven miles across the top of the mountain. This was journey's end, the promised land that Dambom had found twenty-six years ago and longed to visit again to show to his family.

Gossip *in Sundal Bay*.

It was in the summer of 1902 when *Rothion*, with Dambom and Scrase Saxby on board, anchored in Sundal Bay in the same anchorage where *Gossip* now lay. After three stormy days when sailing was impossible a slight improvement in the weather inspired the two young men to activity and they asked Samson Sundal (one of the local fishermen) who had befriended them, to guide them up the mountain and across the Folgëfonni to Odda, thus cutting off the other arm of the Hardanger fjord and avoiding a sea passage of twenty miles.

The sun shone as they toiled up the mountain but clouded over when they reached the snowline at 4,500 feet. The experienced guide surveyed the field of snow ahead.

'Too mox snow,' he said and turned and faced the downward track.

Dambom and Scrase were young and eager and not to be put off so easily. After a little persuasion Sundal, no longer a young man, agreed to lead them. The virgin snow was deep and crusty and they sank knee deep at every step. After half an hour the light mist turned to fog. Sundal was flagging and said he had had enough. Dambom then took the small cardboard compass and armed with the ship's boat-hook took the lead and broke the trail. Each step was an effort, nothing was to be seen, they might have been crossing the Arctic Circle. Another half-hour passed and even Dambom looked white and drawn. Scrase then took the little compass and Sundal trudged behind them shuffling along in the trodden snow. The two young men took turns of leading, the old one followed, silent and stubborn. Dambom found it difficult to tell if they were going up hill or down, but at one stage he felt the going was slightly easier. Suddenly the fog cleared completely and they saw the whole of the Hardanger fjord, with its small twinkling islands, laid out below them in bright sunlight. The snow was all around them but Sundal recovered enough to take charge once more and was able to pick out the beacons and guide them down to the village of Odda. He had booked them in at the local hotel where they arrived frozen and exhausted but were soon revived by brandy, hot baths and food.

They had all recovered by the next morning and Sundal and a friend rowed the two pioneers three miles down the fjord to the pier where they caught a steamer back to the bay where *Rothion* awaited them on the other side of the mountain.

It seemed only natural that now, twenty-six years later, when we went ashore, our first objective was to call on old Samson Sundal. The old man, very, very old he seemed to us, welcomed us slowly at first, then with great acclamation when he recognized Dambom and soon the two men were reminiscing about the great trek of 1902. Sundal was a fine-looking man with a flowing white beard, snow-white hair and piercing ice-blue eyes. Bess and I were riveted to him; surely here was the genuine 'Ancient Mariner'.

Before we left, Dambom asked him to find a guide to take the four of us up the mountain and possibly across the Folgëfonni, but here the old man was adamant.

'Up the mountain, but yes, perhaps with a good guide maybe and a pony, but across the snows, never for Madam and the lassies.'

The mate heartily agreed with him and eventually he promised to find a guide and a pony to take us up the mountain.

The next morning dawned brilliantly clear, and with our picnic lunch we met the guide and his lovely cream-coloured Norwegian pony on the quay at nine o'clock. The early part of the climb was easy but we enjoyed taking turns on Pömp, the surefooted pony who climbed over the rocky terrain with never a false step. We went close to the Bondhusbrae glacier and saw the caves underneath the ice, bright blue and green like frozen peacock's breasts.

It was midday when we reached the snowline and here the going was slippery, especially for Bess and me shod only in sandshoes, and Pömp became even

more popular. When we reached the rest hut at 4,500
feet we were glad of the shelter and ate our
sandwiches huddled together on the seat inside. A
little goat which had attached itself to us on the way
up came in with us he was so greedy and cheeky that
after feeding him on our crusts we had to shut him
outside with the pony.

After lunch we stood in the snow and gazed across
the Folgëfonni which stretched ahead in never ending
folds of pure white plumes. Far, far below we could
see *Gossip* alone in the bay resembling a toy yacht in
a rock pool and beyond her a peep of the open sea
between the granite islands.

The descent was difficult at times and there was one
frightening place where a bottomless crevasse had
formed in the snow. We had crossed over it on the
way up and found it hazardous enough but now we
dreaded it even more as we had had time to imagine
what would happen if any one of us had slipped and
been swallowed up by the icy, beckoning, chasm.
Pömp and the men made light of it and Nickel (as we
had christened the little goat) skipped happily over
the, gap, but the mate found it terrifying and I
certainly jibbed at it although in reality the gap was
very narrow and I might even have lodged in the top!

We arrived back in Sundal in the evening very tired
but with a feeling of achievement as we looked up at
the great glacier gleaming rosy-red in the Norwegian
twilight.

We had come nearly 500 miles from Göteborg in
sixteen days with adverse weather conditions and we
now planned to sail 600 miles back to Svendborg in
Denmark in twenty days. It seemed a reasonable plan
but it proved to be quite hard sailing as we had more
head winds and bad weather when rounding
Jaederens-Rev and the Naze.

We had bad luck when on August 31st, just a mile
and a half from Frederiksvaern, the wind failed and
the engine refused to start. Dambom, thoroughly
disgruntled, turned in below to read his detective

story - a habit he was addicted to in times of
frustration when nothing could be done - and left
Bess and me to cope on our own. He fell asleep and
was delighted when he was roused two hours later,
by the sound of the anchor chain, to find *Gossip* was
safely anchored in her old berth in the harbour.

We didn't think Dambom really meant us to bring
Gossip into harbour on our own, but Bess said she
remembered the entrance and after a short scrutiny of
the chart she took command. I was steering as usual
and under her guidance, with the lightest of airs, we
sailed so quietly into the large natural harbour that
the guns never stirred from the rocks, perhaps
thinking that the white yacht was some giant
albatross gliding on the water. It was only after I had
luffed up into the wind that the silence was broken as
Bess threw the anchor over the bow and the chain
rattled through the fairlead into the still water.

We now had 400 miles to make in eight days, quite
a tall order. After dining ashore that evening we
came on board and watched the enormous moon
climbing behind the crags of Starvaso. It looked most
alluring and at last the wind was fair, so Dambom
suggested a night passage to Sweden. We all agreed
and Bess and I were full of enthusiasm at the thought
of spending such a lovely night at sea.

By ten o'clock we were sailing out of the harbour
guided by the lights in line astern. Dambom laid a
course to clear the Koster Islands and left Bess and
me to take the first watch. I took the wheel and Bess
studied the charts and tried to identify the various
lights. We were really in charge and enjoying
ourselves with big mugs of hot cocoa and a steady
supply of biscuits and chocolate. We met a number
of ships crossing the Oslo fjord and were very careful
to watch their navigation lights. We repeated the old
adage every time we saw one coming towards us.

When both lights you see ahead
Starboard wheel, and show your Red. (two yachts meeting)
Green to Green-or Red to Red (two yachts passing)
Perfect safety-go ahead!
If to your starboard Red appear,
'Tis your duty to keep clear;
To act as judgement says is proper
To Port-or Starboard-Back or, Stop her!
But when upon your port is seen
A steamer's starboard light of Green
There's not so much for you to do,
For Green to port keeps clear of you. (Two ships crossing)
Both in safety and in doubt
Always keep a good lookout;
In danger, with no room to turn, Ease her! Stop her! Go
astern!

Dambom came on deck once during our watch, then seeing all was well he left us steering on our old friend Torbjörnskjer. As we approached the lighthouse at two in the morning, he took over and we crawled into our warm bunks.

We reached Marstrand at seven o'clock that evening after a splendid sail covering 103 miles from Frederiksvaern.

A week later we reached Svendborg having spent one day storm bound in Copenhagen and two more well reefed down in strong winds. The sound was quiet and peaceful when we sailed in and drifted slowly towards the old wharf at Hestehauge, where we moored *Gossip* in her final resting place for the winter after a cruise covering 1,123 miles in just over five weeks.

The Webers recognized *Gossip* as she sailed in and were ready to greet us when we landed. We worked hard next day laying up our gear in the store and cleaning the ship. Mr. Weber was most helpful and we felt very glad that we had decided to come back to his yard. He had just built himself a motor-glider

capable of doing thirty-six knots and he took us, each
in turn in this tiny boat and gave us a spin up the
sound to Svendborg. Two miles in four minutes!
Later we had tea in his charming house on the sound
and next morning he saw us off on our journey back
to Esbjerg where we boarded the *M.S. Parkstone*
bound for Harwich.

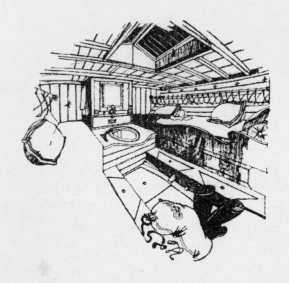

1929 – 31 – Voyage Home and the Schneider Trophy Contest

In June the following year Dambom, with his great friend Colonel Kindersley, and Lionel Landon, who had sailed in *Gossip* from Stockholm to Göteborg in 1927, while a Cambridge undergraduate, went out to Svendborg to sail *Gossip* the 600 miles back to her home waters in the Solent. They accomplished this passage in thirteen days in spite of spending four days storm bound early on in the voyage.

From Svendborg they crossed Kiel Bay with a good fair wind, arriving at Holtenau, with its twin locks at the entrance of the Kiel Canal, late in the evening. Lights were blazing in a variety of colours and not comprehending their significance, Dambom took a chance and steered *Gossip* into the nearest lock hoping to get the first tow the following morning. Shouts of abuse in a deep guttural voice soon made it obvious that he had chosen the wrong course, and

they were bustled out into the great basin where they
lay alongside the wall. This was wrong again, so they
crossed to the other side of the basin, where slowly
and irrevocably the pontoon slid into position,
shutting out the Baltic behind them.

In former times, when Dambom had come through
the canal in Rothion, he had been marshalled into
position on the night before he required the tow,
when as many as ten vessels, two abreast, were fined
up in formation and attached to a single tug which set
off at dawn to take its miscellany of little ships the
sixty miles through the canal to Brunsbüttel.

This time, however, they had to wait several hours
on the following morning before a suitable tug could
be found. Eventually they chartered the *Grechen*, a
ketch-rigged coaster, which towed them all day
through the long dreary canal in the hot sun for the
sum of twenty marks.

They reached Cuxhaven the next evening, and there
they stayed for four depressing days while the
westerly gales moaned overhead, the rain fell, and
the glass dropped steadily day by day.

During this time of enforced inaction Dambom and
his crew walked each morning to the dyke above the
River Elbe to visit the 'Borkum Arms'. One might
assume that they were drowning their sorrows in
good German ale, but in reality the 'Borkum Arms'
is a tall weather indicator bearing two dials slung on
vertical wires labelled 'B' and 'H', and on each dial
an arrow or indicator showing the direction of the
wind at Borkum and Heligoland respectively. Above
this, on the central standard, there are semaphore
arms indicating the force of wind at 'B' or 'H' on the
ratio of one arm to two points on the Beaufort Scale.
Hence the 'Borkum Arms'.

One day five arms appeared for Heligoland
indicating Force 9 or 10 and there were never less
than three.

They eventually left Cuxhaven on a morning when
the glass was still low but the north-west wind only
moderate. Trying to make up for lost time they made
the long passage to Helder (183 miles) without a
further pause. All went well until late that evening.
They had crossed the Terschelling estuary and
Dambom picked out a bright flashing light which he
took to be the Helder. The compass, owing to some
chemical action, had darkened over and was
fatiguing to steer by so the bright light was very
welcome. The wind dropped at midnight, so
Dambom started the engine, and almost at once an
ominous shudder ran through the ship as her keel
bumped on the bottom in the heavy swell. On deck,
breakers could be heard roaring up the sandy beach.
They gybed at once away from the beckoning light.
A sounding showed two fathoms. Then slowly and
steadily, as Lionel swung the lead, he called out
three, three and a half, four, and then five fathoms as
the noise of the breakers decreased astern. Dambom
was really puzzled and set to work to check the lights
with the chart. It was then that he discovered that he
had mistaken the Texel Island light, a new
installation since his last visit, for the true Helder
light and *Gossip* was actually trying to sail between a
shoal and the Island!

Dambom blamed himself for this grave mistake,
terming it an act of gross carelessness, bred of
fatigue, in not checking the new course on the chart.

After this little misunderstanding *Gossip* entered
the Nieu Diep Canal at Den Helder, the headquarters
of the Dutch Navy at eight o'clock and tied up
alongside the wharf in a gap between two cruisers.
Dambom at once retired to his bunk having had only
four hours' sleep since leaving Cuxhaven at dawn the
previous day. The crew, who had managed to get
more sleep than the skipper, made off with indecent
haste to the best hotel in the place for a much needed
breakfast. Two hours later they came on board again,
trampling noisily over the decks, extolling in loud

voices the excellence of the meal they had just
devoured. On Dambom's enquiry as to whether any
provision had been made for the poor 'worker' of the
party, even if his last night's work had not been of a
very high standard, they unblushingly replied that at
half past twelve another even more substantial meal
would be awaiting all three of them.

After a really satisfying lunch and hospitality from
the friendly Dutch Navy, whose premises they had
invaded by mistake, they were on board again by two
o'clock and as the fair north-east breeze was still
blowing they set sail immediately. They made
Ymuiden that evening and all enjoyed a long night's
sleep.

The following day they sailed along the Dutch coast
past the mouths of the Rhine and the Maas which
open up the great waterways of Holland. The wind
freshened in the evening and the crew put two reefs
in the mainsail to ease the steering. By two o'clock
in the morning, it was blowing a Force 8 gale and
they reefed down again until only two hoops
remained on the mast. With the sea abeam it was
necessary for the helmsman to run *Gossip* off every
now and again when the waves got really big. She
was averaging six and a half knots in spite of the
reduced sail and the steepness of the seas.

At half past one Dambom spotted the flash of
Ostend's great light in the sky and soon he was able
to pick out the Wenduine Light Vessel.
Unfortunately they had to give the Wenduine shoal a
wide berth and so got to leeward of Ostend. This
meant a weary thrash to windward to fetch the pier-
head and it was a quarter past four and daylight
before they were able to drop anchor off the Yacht
Club in the midst of a fleet of 12-metres.

Next day sturdy old *Gossip* extricated herself from
her anchorage where she lay surrounded by the
graceful swan-like 12-metres, who were dressed
overall awaiting the local regatta. Leaving them to

their racing she sailed to Dunkerque with a fair wind
and from there crossed to Folkestone and continued
along the south coast without a pause until she
reached Cowes where they anchored for an hour to
clear Customs before sailing home to Yarmouth. The
500 miles from Cuxhaven to Yarmouth had taken
them six days.

Claude Worth, Commodore of the Royal Cruising
Club, writing in the journal that year, remarked that
Gossip's cruise was nearly brought to an abrupt end
off Texel Island, and added:

'Those of us who have had a similar narrow escape
are the better for it, for the lesson is likely to last a
lifetime.'

It was lovely to have *Gossip* home again after her
four years in the Baltic and we sailed in her a great
deal around the Solent during the next two years.
Dambom enjoyed everything, whether it was
watching the fireworks at the end of Cowes week and
sailing back in the dark, or a Scouts' outing, when
half the boys were sick and the other half asked
innumerable questions, or a day's expedition to the
Hamble where we anchored close to the strawberry
fields, and spent two hours ashore picking as much
fruit as we could for the modest sum of half a crown,
before rowing back to the yacht with dozens of little
baskets full of ripe strawberries, ready for the annual
jam-making session. Whenever a Naval Review or
any special function took place off Portsmouth or
Cowes, *Gossip* was sure to be in the thick of it with a
good crowd of happy people on board, feasting,
merrymaking, sometimes vomiting, but all enjoying
themselves, at least most of the time.

During these years we had our own mooring up the
River Yar, opposite the old mill, in one of the
prettiest reaches of the river. Dambom, with the aid
of the girls of course, always laid his own moorings.

This wasn't a difficult task, but thinking back on it now I realize that it was a more suitable occupation for men than girls. First, Dambom would select two strong elm saplings from the garden and cut them into sturdy posts with tapered ends. Then, armed with two lengths of chain, one very heavy, the other slightly lighter, a sledge-hammer, an assortment of shackles, a mooring buoy, various tools and two daughters, he would set off in the dinghy at dead low water springs. When he reached his chosen spot he would disembark, hammer in one of the stakes and affix the heavy cable, or ground chain, to its base. We then had to measure out the ground chain until we reached its centre, when Dambom would shackle on the lighter bridle chain. Leaving this for one daughter to hold, he would cross the river in the dinghy with the second stake, the rest of the paraphernalia and the second available daughter whose duty it was to pay out the ground chain as he rowed across. After the second stake had been fixed in position and the chain attached, it only remained to collect the first daughter who was still clutching the bridle, and adjust this with the mooring buoy attached in the middle of the river.

Dambom was apt to make a false economy with the mooring buoy by insisting on using one of his own making. This consisted of a number of pieces of cork, found by beachcombing, impaled on small pointed sticks and covered with a coat of hand-sewn canvas. Sometimes these creations became waterlogged and sank, and sometimes they were tom apart by general wear and tear. When they were lost we had to grapple along the river bed, at dead low water, to find the ground chain and bridle on which to attach a new buoy.

On the occasions when we laid our mooring off the Yacht Club, the same principle was employed with two very heavy anchors taking the place of the elm stakes. This operation was slightly easier as it all took place from the dinghy and had the advantage of only requiring one daughter as assistant.

Lying up the river was by far the most pleasant anchorage but it meant that every time we went out, dear old Mr. Doe, the much revered harbour master, had to stop all the traffic on the main road and open the swing-span bridge to let us through. We always warned him when we were going out, though with our erratic engine we were often a little inaccurate in our judgment, but the return journey was much more difficult as we could give no warning until we reached the harbour mouth and then the shrill blast of our foghorn would send him bustling along from the quay to the controls on the bridge. In all the years when we lived up the river he never once let us down, nor did he ever complain of the extra work we must have given him.

Perhaps the most exciting events we attended in *Gossip* were the Schneider Trophy races which took place in 1929 and 1931. These contests were bi-annual affairs open to seaplanes of all nations. As Britain had been the winner in Venice in 1927 the next race was destined to be in British waters, and the Solent was selected as being the most suitable area.

Early on the morning of September 7th 1929, *Gossip* sailed out of Yarmouth Harbour with a large party of family and friends on board. It was a fine clear day and everyone was in high spirits.

The course formed a quadrilateral with the four pylons marking the turning points off Seaview, Hayling Island, Southsea and West Cowes. We took up our anchorage in a strategic position in Osborne Bay off East Cowes. Lunch was served on deck as there was so much to see before the start with the constant movement of the paddle-steamers, the rescue launches, the naval patrols and yachts of all shapes and sizes.

Only two teams were entered, the British and the Italians. The French team had withdrawn three weeks

before the contest and misfortune hit the only
American entry who was severely injured in a
preliminary test.

By half past one all shipping in the vicinity was
stopped with the exception of the patrol boats and the
rescue launches and half an hour later we all
assembled on deck or sat straddling the boom
awaiting the start.

Promptly at two o'clock the first British contestant,
Flying Officer Waghorn, flew over from Calshot in
his shining blue and white Rolls-Royce Supermarine
and scorched across the starting-line at Ryde pier-
head. Almost at once the sun flashed on his fuselage
as he rounded the pylon off Seaview and we heard
the steady roar of his engine as he zoomed round the
course. This became almost deafening as he
approached our anchorage and surged overhead to
finish his first round. I had just remembered to flick
on the stop-watch so that we were able to check the
speed of his lap.

The next competitor was an Italian in a Macchi and
again I checked the time on the stop-watch, but he
cut the sharp hairpin turning point at East Cowes so
fine that he lost speed and seemed so shaken that he
swerved low over *Gossip* screeching like a dying
banshee as he cleared our mast by inches. There was
a radio commentator on Ryde Pier reporting on the
race and the next minute, as the wild Italian flew low
over the water towards him, we heard him shout over
the air:

'This chap's coming pretty low-by Jove he is
coming low
-Good Lord he's going to hit us!'

British and Italian planes took alternative rounds
with three entries each.

One of our pilots missed out a mark and was
disqualified, and 'Monti', the third Italian pilot, met
with disaster. As he screeched over our anchorage on

his second round, we were horrified to see a plume of black smoke spurting from the exhaust of his blood-red Macchi. As it lost height and plunged towards the sea it appeared to be on fire but with fantastic control the pilot checked his headlong descent and alighted on the water off Seaview, where he was immediately rescued by the crew of one of the R.A.F. launches.

The final result was a win to Britain for Wing Commander Orlebar's 'High Speed Flight', with Flying Officer Waghorn the overall winner with a speed of 328.63 m.p.h.

Britain, with two successive wins, now only needed to do the 'hat trick' to become the permanent holder of the Trophy. Unfortunately the outlook seemed very black when the British Government withheld their support for the 1931 contest. However, a fairy godmother appeared in the guise of Lady Houston, who saved the day by financing the whole project and with only seven months in which to prepare a new plane, Vickers and Rolls-Royce produced the *Supermarine S6B*, which was a more powerful edition of the model used by the winning pilot in 1929.

On September 12th 1931, *Gossip* with the entire family and several friends on board, left Yarmouth on a cool breezy morning to take up her position on the course.

Four-year-old Alan, with his governess Luki (the long-suffering successor to Dicky), was much in evidence and amongst the guests was a very pretty girl who came on board dressed in a flowered cotton frock and a big floppy picture hat, more suitable for Ascot than for sailing in the Solent. Bess and I, clad in our shapeless skirts and well-worn jerseys, were secretly rather envious of her, but we were so busy hoisting the sails and helping with the running of the ship that we had little time for our own thoughts. It soon became clear that conditions weren't ideal for a day at sea with a large party, and within minutes of meeting the choppy seas of the Solent, 'Floppy Hat' and Luki had taken up their respective positions in

the port and starboard bunks in the aftercabin and
weren't seen on deck again until the end of the day.

The course that year was a triangular one, with the
turning points at Ryde Middle, West Wittering and
St. Helens, and so we had to sail eastward of Cowes
in order to get a reasonable view of the race. We
sailed past the crowded beaches where some of the
people had been camping out all night and anchored
between Fishbourne and Ryde. It was only then that
we heard from one of the patrol boats that the contest
had been postponed for twenty-four hours owing to
unfavourable weather conditions. It was just twelve
o' clock so we decided to serve lunch to anyone who
was still well enough to eat it before sailing for
home. My cousin Rowland was sitting on deck, his
face the delicate green of a duck's egg.

'How do you feel?' I asked him.

'I have exactly thirty seconds,' he said. Instantly, if
unkindly, I produced the stop-watch and gave him
the count down. Sure enough, he was accurate to the
second.

The homeward sail was very rough and unpleasant.
As we had a foul tide and a head wind to contend
with and a number of unhappy people on board,
Dambom decided to go into Newtown River for the
night to put them out of their misery. We anchored
close to the small quay and rowed the party ashore in
relays. Everyone was glad to reach land but the
labours of the day were by no means over as we had
to walk five miles back to Yarmouth and some of our
friends, especially 'Floppy Hat' were in no condition
for a country trek. I took Alan under my wing and
sometimes on my back and regaled him with an
endless flow of stories to keep his mind off the long
walk. Never before or since have I invented so many
tales.

The contest was held the following day in
reasonably good weather conditions and once again
Gossip took up her position just clear of the course.

All the family were present and several guests, undaunted by the hardships of the previous day, added to the ship's company.

Unfortunately Britain was the only country represented, as France, Italy and America had all withdrawn.

Flight Lieutenant Boothman, in his *Supermarine S6B*, completed a perfect round for Britain. As he swept gracefully round the sharp turn at Ryde Middle buoy, he roared over our heads, much to young Alan's delight, before crossing the line off Ryde pier-head. We checked the speed of his laps and all cheered when he crossed the finishing line on his last lap to win the Schneider Trophy for Britain with a record speed of 340.08 m.p.h.

One of the most beautiful and spectacular of the annual events which take place in the Solent is the famous 'Round the Island Race' which is organized by the Island Sailing Club. Nowadays the starters in this popular race exceed four hundred and the sight of this fleet answering the gun in the early hours of a July morning is one I look forward to from year to year. Although the yachts are divided into two or three classes starting at ten-minute intervals, the sight an hour or so after the first gun, is of a blue sea speckled with sailing ships stretching in an unbroken ribbon of coloured canvas from Cowes to Yarmouth. The only sounds to be heard are the whining of the winches, the impatient flapping of the headsails and the strident calls for 'water' as the yachts tack, and tack again close inshore trying to cheat the foul tide.

The prevailing winds are the westerlies, so it is invariably a windward start but as the yachts round the Needles and alter course for St. Catherine's Point, they gybe round and ease their sheets and then comes the most wonderful sight of the day, when the great billowing spinnakers break forth in a kaleidoscope of colours and the fleet gathers speed like a fantasy of tropical swans on a blue lagoon.

The very first of these races was held on July 11th 1931, and *Gossip*, with Dambom, Bess and several friends on board was one of the original twenty-one starters. It was a very friendly affair and almost a family concern for the Ratseys who entered their three yachts, *Harrier*, *Daedalus* and the picturesque *Dolly Varden*, with her long bowsprit, blue hull and copper-coloured sails.

Gossip in the first Round the Island Race.

Gossip made a reasonable start but when she tacked to clear the Squadron rocks, Dambom had to climb the mast by the mainsail hoops to adjust the topsail sheet which was foul of the main halyard.

The first part of the race through the Solent was quite exciting with most of the yachts fairly close together and *Gossip* well up with the leaders but the wind dropped as they reached Freshwater Bay and the fleet became scattered, the inshore boats losing the wind completely under the lee of the land. Darkness fell before they finished but all the yachts completed the course and were checked in at the Island Sailing Club. *Merry Conceit* was the first winner on corrected time and so Peter Brett became the first holder of the coveted Gold Roman Bowl. *Harrier*, owned by Tom Ratsey, was second and *Chiquita third. Gossip* finished nineteenth. It was an historic race and the list of yachts taking part was posted on a beam of the Island Sailing Club and remained there until the new premises were built a few years ago.

Dambom was usually very tolerant of the many friends we invited to sail with us, but Bess made a big mistake when she planned a day trip to Bournemouth so that she and her friend Jocelyn could enjoy an afternoon's skating. The day started badly when Jocelyn, who was staying at Norlands, appeared at breakfast in a very attractive if somewhat music-hall version of a sailor-suit. Dambom took one look at the frilly skirt bound with white braid and the white-fronted top with its large square collar and roared with laughter but later when she added a saucy little hat with a white bobby-dazzle to complete the outfit he refused to walk down the road with her to the sand-house where he kept the dinghy.

All might have gone well but as so often in the best-planned sails, the wind was so light after they cleared the Needles channel and their progress so slow that by the time they reached Bournemouth it was time to turn back in order to catch the flood tide in the Solent. This so annoyed Jocelyn that she argued and complained and said she couldn't see why after coming all that way she couldn't go ashore. Finally Dambom became so enraged by her endless chatter that he pulled the dinghy alongside and told her to

get into it and stay there until they reached harbour.
As an after-thought he threw in her knitting, so for
the two hours of the return journey she sat in the
stern of the dinghy, resplendent in her sailor-suit and
saucy hat, calmly knitting while Dambom and Bess
sailed home in silence.

1932 – St. Malo and the Channel Islands

After a year's idling in the Solent, *Gossip* and her skipper felt the urge to seek new waters. On this occasion Dambom crossed to Guernsey with two friends where he was joined by his wife and three daughters who then took over the ship.

We had decided beforehand that this was to be a leisurely cruise, something in the style of Tennyson's Lotus Eaters, when time was of no account and we could wander where we liked.

'Why should we toil, the roof and crown of things?
... Is there any peace
in ever climbing up the climbing wave?
Surely, surely slumber is more sweet than toil, the shore
Than labour in the deep mid-ocean, wind and wave and oar.'

The mate, Bess and I felt we would welcome more time in which to explore the new lands we visited, perhaps as a reaction to our rather strenuous cruises in Scandinavia, and Lucia - aged eleven - was so thrilled at the thought of her first trip abroad, that nothing else really mattered. She was so excited that she wouldn't say the magic word 'France' in case it broke the spell and she never reached her dream-land, but spoke only of 'F' in bated breath.

With this idea in mind, Dambom entertained his all female crew to dinner at Old Government House Hotel, overlooking the harbour, when we arrived by steamer at St. Peter Port.

We spent our first day in Guernsey visiting the Channel Islands Yacht Club, climbing the steps to the market where we bought fresh fish, local grown tomatoes and thick clotted cream,, and walking along the quay to Castle Cornet, the great fortress guarding the entrance to the port.

We hoped to explore Sark next morning but as we sailed up to the little island of Jethou in a light easterly wind, the tide in the Grand Russel proved too strong, so after coasting round Little Sark we bore away for Jersey in the fair tide. The rugged rocks of the Paternoster group stood out like a maze of underwater cathedrals, the spires just clear above the waves. We gave them a good berth and with Les Ecrehou rocks on our port side, came round the north-east coast of Jersey and opened Mount Orgueil Castle, the massive stronghold towering over Gorey. This little harbour dries out at low water, so after mooring *Gossip* alongside the quay we ranged our chain cable along the scuppers on the near side to ensure a good list. We then attached the kedge anchor to the topsail halyard, which ran through the block before being made fast to a bollard on the quay, thus making a dangling flexible weight to keep her against the wall. This proved to be a most successful arrangement and she grounded and re-floated again without any further attention. We used this method of Dambom's whenever we lay alongside a quay.

Next day, after visiting Mount Orgueil Castle, all hands turned to and scrubbed *Gossip* as she lay high and dry on the clean sandy bottom. We slapped on a coat of anti-fouling and just completed the task as the tide came in and lapped our feet.

We stayed three days in Jersey, walking, swimming and even going by bus to St. Helier and St. Aubins. We thought the latter a charming little harbour, although quite half a mile from the sea at low water, and decided to lie there next time we visited the island.

Lucia's great day came at last when we sailed from Gorey and headed towards France. It was a still day, with fog hanging in patches over the sea, and mirages, which appeared suddenly when the fog lifted. At one time Les Iles Chausey seemed to be close ahead, but this proved to be an optical illusion in the strange half-light as moments later they took up their rightful position - several miles away. It was all weirdly disconcerting and when we joined up with the French fishing fleet, with their vivid-coloured sails, the masts were raked at such an angle that they appeared to be on their beam ends in the flat calm. We thought this was another illusion until we saw them later that evening in harbour.

We entered the 'avant port' of Granville, and seeing the lockgates open, went straight into the inner basin and made fast alongside the quay. The lock-gates shut behind us and we were imprisoned in the fetid pool. The heat was intense. The air pregnant with refuse from the fishing fleet. Even the gulls, feebly squawking for the entrails, seemed lethargic. Poor Lucia. So this was 'F'! All her illusions were shattered. She climbed ashore and stood on the quay listening to the foreign language. Even this was disappointing. She didn't understand a word of the fishermen's jargon. She returned to *Gossip* dulled by disappointment.

One night in Granville was more than enough for all of us. Lucia and I spent the night on deck rather than swelter in the suffocating saloon. We were awakened at seven o'clock by a Customs official who asked for 'Le Maître'.

I shammed sleep but Lucia sat up in her pyjamas. Here at last was a word she knew.

'"Le Maître", he sleep, sleep, sleep,' she said and put her head back on the pillow in dumb show.

It worked. We were left in peace for another two hours by which time 'Le Maître' was up and ready to see him.

After visiting the 'Douanes' for the ship's passport and shopping in the town - an exhausting performance with the thermometer registering 87°F - we sailed for Les Iles Chausey. There was very little wind and we had to start the engine to clear the harbour but the distance was only a few miles and by mid-morning we were in the Sound of Chausey poring over our ancient French chart trying to sort out the tangle of islands.

We came in at high-water springs and were lucky enough to find a quiet anchorage in a deep pool near the Grande Ile. There were several islands and rocks standing out in the archipelago when we arrived but I don't think that any one of us was prepared for the strange formation which took place before our eyes as we ate our lunch on deck. Islands and rocks were apparently growing out of the water and closing in around us. One minute a clear pool of water, and within an hour a circle of rocks in the same pool and a sandy beach already gleaming white in the sunshine. It was as though we had entered into a giant's bath tub, and for a joke he had pulled out the plug and left acres of rocks and sand and a whole fleet of little white fishing boats marooned high and dry, far from the water's edge.

Les Iles Chausey have perhaps the greatest range of tide found in European waters but in spite of this the actual tidal stream is no greater than that of the Petit Russel or the Swinge which sweep round Guernsey and Alderney.

At low water the great prawning net did a splendid job and Dambom helped us to get the greatest catch of all times. The water was so warm that we stayed

in the sea until the giant prepared to gather in the
waters again for his evening bath.

From Les Iles Chausey we sailed to St. Malo on a
perfect day, sunny and clear and without the intense
heat of the last few days. The entrance to the gulf of
St. Malo is most attractive with its islands and
ancient fortresses. We anchored off the Yacht Club at
Dinard and almost at once a boat came alongside and
the owner invited us to become honorary members of
the club during our visit. We found this a most
friendly place when we accepted their invitation and
had tea there that afternoon.

From St. Malo we continued on our leisurely way
visiting some of the beautiful rivers of the Côtes du
Nord. We hoped to visit Paimpol, the little oyster-
fishing port which dries out completely at low water
but according to the chart we could only reach it at
high-water springs, so after negotiating our way
through the Anse de Paimpol, a wide expanse of
water marked with an alarming array of black and
white towers, we entered the Ile Blanche channel
leading into the Rade de Brehat. Bess and Dambom
between them worked out our route, marking each
rock and beacon on the chart as we closed it. At one
time the pilotage was so involved that I had to put
the ship about three times while they sorted it out.
Eventually we entered the Rade de Brehat which was
marked with great towers and 'bolises' like a street
in a built-up area. This course took us into the lovely
Trieux River which we followed through wooded
cliffs to the little village of Lézardrieux.

After visiting the village and buying some of the
local oysters, we moved *Gossip* from her berth below
the quay to a little bay half a mile down the river
close to the starboard-hand mark, Le Peadrix. Of all
the anchorages where *Gossip* has rested in France
this is my favourite. At night in the quiet pool under
the watchful green eye of Le Peadrix, the only
sounds that break the silence are the rich plaintive
calls of the oyster-catchers, redshanks and curlews as

they fly to fresh feeding grounds; and in the woods above the cliffs a hooting owl or the short bark of a fox betrays the existence of the wild birds and beasts who live their secret lives undisturbed by man.

The Jaudy River can be reached from the Trieux River through the Gaine channel, but when we set out to take this course next morning there was a slight haze and the marks were difficult to distinguish, so we took the safer course going three miles out to La Jument buoy. This buoy lies close to the tall lighthouse of Les Héaux and from there we sailed up seven miles of wild rockbound river to the anchorage below the town of Tréguier, where the stately granite cathedral, with its intricate open-work spire, stands like a monarch enthroned on the hill.

Next morning Bess left us to return to England. After seeing her off Dambom and I hoisted the dinghy on deck, with the aid of the peak halyard and once clear of La Corne - the sturdy beacon lighthouse in the river - we hoisted the topsail. We could just lay the course for Guernsey and I settled down to my usual place at the wheel. After four hours I picked out the great tapering tower of the terrible Douvres where Gilliat allegedly spent his three months' lonely vigil. The wind freshened as we neared the rocks and we had a splendid sail doing seven knots with our scuppers awash. By eight o'clock that evening we were moored in our usual berth in St. Peter Port.

The next day being Lucia's birthday, Dambom gave her a free hand with the agenda. She pleased us all by choosing a lunch picnic on Sark followed by dinner at Old Government House Hotel on our return to Guernsey.

We left the harbour under motor as there was barely enough wind to fill the sails but with the aid of a fair tide we reached the little anchorage in Banquette Bay, between the high-cliffed islands of Sark and Brecqhou, in less than two hours. The water was so clear that we could see the starfish and stones at the bottom at a depth of two fathoms. We rowed the short distance to the shore over clear blue water which shoaled to emerald-green and ate our lunch on the small pebbly beach beneath the precipitous cliffs.

In the afternoon we climbed the zig-zag path leading up through gorse and heather to the summit. The view from the top was worth all the exertion of the climb as we saw our beloved *Gossip*, a tiny white ship, alone in the rock-bound bay hundreds of feet below us. This view of the yacht seen from a great height, which we observed several times in Norway, has never ceased to enchant me. I think it must be the miniature perfection of the boat which is enhanced by its loneliness in high surroundings and a feeling of faith in the strength and unity of our family, knowing that, guided by Dambom, we could take that same little ship to any port in the world under sail alone.

From the top of the cliff we walked to La Coupée, along the narrow track, only a few feet wide, which joins the two parts of the island, Sark and Little Sark. Dambom and the mate returned to the dinghy from here being worried about the rising tide but Lucia and I walked round to the eastern side to see the old mill standing above Terrible Bay overlooking the army of menacing rocks and tide overfalls. As we tried to pick out some of the lights and beacons a faint mist drifted in from the west and blurred the sun. Rather alarmed we turned back only to find the mist gathering over the Island. Lucia and I, who lack Dambom's uncanny bump of locality, soon realized that we were well and truly lost on this tiny island which only measures three miles long and a mile and a half across. We wandered desperately in circles. Each path seemed identical and ended at the cliff edge but never at the right one leading down to the bay where *Gossip* awaited us. Eventually some human beings loomed up in the mist and strangely enough I soon recognized them as science mistresses from my school, Wycombe Abbey. They were able to lead us to the cliff above Banquette Bay and we clambered down to the beach to find Dambom really worried as the fog was wafting over the water and he wanted to get under way immediately while there was still a chance of identifying the rocks and beacons. Luckily he had already worked out the compass courses and as soon as we were back on board we hauled up the anchor and left our pretty anchorage, which had become dulled and lifeless in the menacing fog. We motored out of the bay and were soon able to pick out the Muse Beacon south of Jethou but from then on the fog thickened, and we had a worrying time crossing the shipping lane in the Petit Russel before we picked out the great grey blur of Castle Cornet and the entrance lights of St. Peter Port. Lucia, regardless of the tension, managed to catch two large mackerel off Jethou during this short passage whilst I steered and Dambom kept a keen look-out. It was with a feeling of great relief and thankfulness that we celebrated her twelfth birthday with a dinner ashore that evening.

While we were still in the harbour we watched *Gulnare*, one of *Gossip*'s contemporaries, sail in and anchor close beside us. The owner, Donald Cree, a founder member and secretary of the Royal Cruising Club, acknowledged our hail and rowed across to visit us as soon as he was safely moored with his sails neatly stowed. Donald was always a welcome guest, especially with Lucia, whom he christened 'The Rat' from the habit she had of darting about the ship and reappearing up hatchways and down the rigging in the most unexpected way. We all loved listening to his yarns, some of which sounded highly improbable but which he related with a perpetual twinkle in his blue eyes.

After a further two days in the Channel Islands, on one of which we visited Herm - the fairy island with the shell beach, where we gathered cowries - we left Guernsey with a moderate westerly wind for our passage home to the Isle of Wight.

With the topsail set we cleared the Casquets in two and a half hours, logging a good seven knots.

Unfortunately the wind freshened here and we had to
hand the topsail and by six o'clock the sea was lumpy
and the sky clouding over. There is always a certain
amount of excitement and anxiety about making a
landfall after a longish passage by dead reckoning, so
when the log recorded fifty-five miles out of the sixty
from the Casquets to the Needles, with no sign of
land, Dambom began to get really worried. I had done
an eight-hour spell at the wheel (entirely by choice)
when my father took over from me, keeping her head
north-east before the wind, feeling sure that we were
to windward of the Bill. Presently he spotted a dark
murky bank to starboard which resolved itself into
some high land and almost immediately Portland Bill
lighthouse loomed up not two miles away but most
unfortunately on the wrong side. This was the first
time I had known Dambom make a bad landfall.
Perhaps I was at fault with the steering. Perhaps we
had misjudged the strength of the west-going tide; in
any case we paid dearly for our mistake. For the next
two hours *Gossip* was held in the strong tide and the
turbulent waters off the most dreaded headland of the
British coast. The calmest water is said to be close in
shore, between The Race and The Bill, well inside
the Shambles reef I tried to hold the ship in this area
but the rising wind fighting against the tide made the
whole sea wild with conflicting waves. This was the
only occasion on board our sturdy ship when I saw
Dambom tie a rope round himself and lash it to the
mast when he had to go forward to put more reefs in
the mainsail. I secured myself with a rope round the
wheel shaft and was thankful for the experience I had
had off the Naze of Norway and Jaederens-Rev, with
the maelstroms I had steered through on those
occasions. This was infinitely more alarming;
infinitely more dangerous. For two hours I never left
the wheel. I was concentrating the whole time;
watching the waves and steering with every nerve
tensed, my knees gripping the wheel-locker, as
Dambom tended the sails and the mate kept her feet

pressed on top of Lucia who was made to curl up in the well of the cockpit until, sodden and crushed, she sought refuge in the mate's bunk where she actually slept! Wave after wave drenched us but the cockpit was self-draining and the seas that surged over the coaming gulped and gurgled their way out again through the scuppers. The bowsprit dipped in the breakers every few seconds, then bounced up again showering spray over the fore-deck and all the time the seas ranted and roared around us making speech almost impossible as we stood our ground, held in the tide, only a cable's length from the rocks. Darkness came. The pulpit rock melted in the gloom, but overhead the beam from the lighthouse illuminated the scene around us, flashing four times, then plunging us into darkness for sixteen seconds, then again four flashes, and darkness, until the tide slackened and we edged round the point. Then the red sector shone out warning us of the Shambles and the light flashes changed their frequency showing us our position on the chart as we sailed close to the eastern shore of the Bill and through the well-lit entrance to Portland harbour, where we moored close to some destroyers. Cold, wet, hungry and exhausted I lit 'blue flame' and heated up some beef stew for dinner but the mate was unable to swallow anything. She told us afterwards that her stomach had become paralysed from fright and it was twelve hours before her tensed-up muscles relaxed and she was able to swallow.

We had a noisy night as the wind increased to gale force and kicked up a nasty sea in the large harbour, making us feel so uncomfortable that as soon as it was light, in spite of the wind and fog which now added to our misery, we felt our way out of Portland under staysail and followed the ferry into Weymouth harbour, where we spent two days storm bound before sailing to the Needles and our home port.

1933-39 – Holland and Anthea

In 1933 *Gossip* was fitted with a secondhand Brooks engine, slightly more powerful than the little 'Day' which had helped us round Scandinavia, but with a strong aversion to going into reverse, which detracted from its value when manoeuvring in harbour. It also took up more room than the tiny 'Day', and although the major works were tucked away under the companionway, the asbestos-lagged exhaust pipe took up a large area of the after-cabin floor space. The carpet had to be taken up when the engine was running, revealing the pipe, which lay like a giant cobra, motionless along the floor. Once after a brief session below in a rough sea, I went on deck complaining that I had burnt my bare toes, but my cousin, Ronald Saxby, who always liked to better me in an argument said:

'Have you ever had to stand at the loo with *Gossip* rolling in a heavy sea?'

When I meekly admitted that I had never tried that approach, he said:

'Well I have. I've stood on the pipe after losing my balance and believe me it produces a cloud of steam and bad language!'

As soon as the engine was fitted we sailed for Holland, coasting along from Spithead to Dover from where we crossed to Calais. We continued in easy stages up the Belgian coast calling at Nieuwpoort, Ostend and Zeebrugge, en route for the busy little port of Flushing, on the Walcheren peninsula, so strategically placed at the great wide estuary of the River Schelde.

There were five of us on board again, all family as in the previous year. Rather too many, we decided, for living in such a small space for weeks on end, so no one was really surprised when Bess suddenly recollected a pressing engagement and left the ship at Flushing.

Holland is a lovely country for leisurely sailing as the whole of the interior can be visited by wandering up and down the rivers and canals.

Middelburg was one of the most attractive towns we visited. We moored alongside the town quay one Sunday morning and watched the women bicycling along the towpath to church in their national dress. their great black billowing skirts in no way affecting their control of the pedals, their starched caps white as snow caught in the morning sun.

Our entry to The Hague was spectacular. We were happily motoring along the canal, our new engine functioning perfectly, when suddenly *Gossip* reared up like a frightened filly and remained poised with her bow rising a good foot out of the water. Apparently, with our lack of knowledge of the Dutch language, we had ignored a notice giving warning of a boom across the canal. The local inhabitants were delighted and turned out in force on foot and on bicycles to enjoy our plight. We laid out a kedge from the dinghy and all hands heaved astern but it was of no avail. Luckily the boys on the towpath came to our aid and thoroughly enjoyed themselves

heaving in unison like a well trained tug-of-war team
until their superior strength prevailed and we slid
backwards into the deep water. As we lay moored
alongside the bank that evening a press photographer
arrived with a presentation copy of the picture he had
taken of '*Gossip* uplifted' which was to appear in the
next day's edition of the local paper.

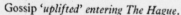

Gossip '*uplifted*' *entering The Hague.*

Other highlights of the trip included a visit to the art
gallery in The Hague where I became enamoured by
'Potters Bull' and an evening spent ashore at Hoorne,
in the Zuider Zee, where Lucia and I bought clogs
and walked up and down the street trying to master
the knack of wearing them until one of the local
inhabitants could bear it no longer and gave us a
lesson in the noble art of clog-walking.

Amsterdam remained in my memory for years and
years mostly, I regret to say, on account of the most
enormous and gormandizical dinner I had ever eaten.
We had run out of food on board and lunch had been
such a paltry meal that Dambom promised us all a
really special dinner ashore that evening. I remember
we entered the splendid hotel clad in our sailing
clothes and were ushered by the head waiter to a
table in the centre of the vast dining-room, where we

took our places amid the amused glances of the élite of the city assembled around us. Course after course was offered. Nothing was refused. Finally - I can see it now - a mountain of cream and meringue, resembling the Taj Mahal, was placed before us. Fresh peaches oozed out of this masterpiece as we attacked it and it tasted scrumptious. Lucia and I emptied our plates. We looked at each other. We looked at the waiter. He came towards us.

'Please could we have some more?' we asked in chorus.

Surely it had never happened before, never had there been such greed. The waiter failed to conceal a smile as he offered us a second replica of the Taj Mahal.

Somehow Lucia and I staggered down the flight of steps from the hotel. Somehow we found our way back to the dinghy. We were suffering as only the greedy can, but oh, how worth while it had been!

This was the last year in which *Gossip* held an unrivalled place in our family for in 1934 Bess and I were lent *Genista*, a half-decked yacht twenty-one feet overall, of the Yarmouth One Design class and we spent the whole of August trailing the fleet of ten, in an endeavour to find out the hard way something about racing. Dambom, although he had always scorned what he called 'racing round the cans' admired our tenacity and enthusiasm and much to our surprise and delight, the next summer he bought *Anthea*, another boat in the same class. He still thought racing rather a senseless pastime but he came out with us on several occasions and sometimes that year we succeeded in moving up a place and even attained a 'third' in a race at Lymington when some of the class sailed the wrong course.

For the next four years Dambom cruised in *Gossip* every year. He usually set off in June making for the Channel Islands and the Brittany coast, or along the south coast westwards to Fowey and the Helford River, returning towards the end of July when the

Yarmouth One Design racing season started and we had to smarten up *Anthea* ready for Cowes.

One year we moored *Gossip* up the Medina River close to the Folly Inn and Dambom, Ronald Saxby - our regular crew - and I lived on board with *Anthea* moored alongside.

We thought it would be a splendid idea just to sail down the river in *Anthea* every morning ready for our class race, with no worry about driving in from Yarmouth every day, parking the car and finding a boatman to take us out to our moorings. The idea was good in theory but in practice it was a dismal failure.

We had to get up even earlier than usual because in the event of a calm we had to row *Anthea* the two miles to the starting line. This wasn't easy as the floating-bridge, plying between East and West Cowes, had to be negotiated - probably two or three times if we were beating or rowing against the tide - and there was a constant movement of shipping as we reached the pontoon. As a result we were often late for the start and, on at least two occasions, we omitted to get our racing instructions in advance and made ourselves very unpopular asking our long-suffering competitors which buoy we were supposed to be rounding. Added to this, when we eventually returned to our moorings after a hard day's racing, we would come on board *Gossip* with wet clothes, wet sails, no food and feeling too exhausted to cope with anything.

After a month spent in racing *Anthea* at Cowes, Lymington and Yarmouth, we always ended the sailing season with a few days' cruising in *Gossip* to Poole or Weymouth or even a quick run across to the Channel Islands, before the culminating week-end in mid-September, when we joined the yachts of the Royal Cruising Club for the annual meet in the Beaulieu River.

1939 was no exception to our routine but much more exciting for us because *Anthea* was in the

running for the coveted Yarmouth One Design
Challenge Cup. Wars and rumours of wars certainly
touched us and odd evenings were even given up to
studying first-aid and anti-gas warfare but the racing
went on as usual.

On August 26th Dambom was called up by the
Territorial Army and Bess had to leave for an
Ambulance Maintenance Course.

This left Lucia and me to sail *Anthea* in the last
vital race. It was vital for us because the Cup was
awarded on points for the number of 'firsts' gained
during the season and if we could get just one more
win, we would tie for first place with *Diatom* and
Magnolia, who already had an equal number of
points.

Bess and Dambom were the regular helmsmen and
Lucia and I had never been allowed to take the boat
on our own before. We were lucky that afternoon
because there was a light westerly wind and, being
only two in the boat instead of the usual three, we
were a light crew. I steered and Lucia crewed single-
handed like one possessed. We led the fleet round
Hurst mark and Lucia set the spinnaker so quickly
and deftly that we increased our lead. Unfortunately
before we reached Lymington Spit buoy there was a
change of wind and we had to gybe. Lucia tried to
gybe the spinnaker over first and in a sudden gust of
wind it slipped out of her hand and caught in the
cross-trees as she was lifting it over. This delayed us
some valuable seconds as I had to gybe again to clear
it and meanwhile, *Katinka*, sailed by Geraldine
Cross, drew ahead of us. Fortunately for us she
slightly misjudged the strength of the tide and by
sailing closer to the Lymington shore we slipped
ahead again and rounded the Spit buoy just inside
her, having established an overlap. We held our lead
across to Bouldnor mark but had a nerve-racking
beat home to the Royal Solent Yacht Club on the last
lap of the course with *Katinka* and two other boats
tacking very close to us. The blessed gun was fired as

we crossed the finishing line only five seconds ahead of *Katinka*.

Lucia and I were elated by our win. I remember every detail of this race even now. I think it is because during the next six years I sailed it over and over again in my second world whenever I wanted to shut out the life around me, and slip backwards into the time before the Germans and the Japs shattered the peace which lay over the land and over the sea and over the quiet waters of the Solent.

The great sail-off for the Cup took place between *Magnolia*, *Diatom* and *Anthea* on August 28th. Bess steered *Anthea* and Lucia and I crewed for her. We were usually a most successful team when we were all three together but alas, on this occasion vanity proved to be our undoing. We had had a riotous and amusing season and a newcomer to the class, known by us as 'Reckless Reggie' - now an eminent politician - had certainly added to the fun. On this all important race he decided to sail round the course in order to take photographs of *Anthea* and her crew. This so distracted us as we found we were always taking sneaking glances astern instead of concentrating on the course ahead, so it was not surprising that *Magnolia* and *Diatom* finished first and second, while *Anthea*, with her foolish, vain crew, was a miserable third.

1939-45 The War Years

Four days later Germany invaded Poland and Dambom rang us up from his depot in Fareham telling us to take *Gossip* up to the yard at Cowes to have her stern gland repaired. I never really discovered what the 'stern gland' consisted of, it was just a name to me rather similar to the 'big end' in a car, desperate when it broke down but otherwise one remained oblivious of its existence. By the time we had mustered a crew for the trip, war had been declared and the same day a splendid white steam yacht *The Star of India* took up her position in the 'roads' outside Yarmouth Harbour, to act as examination vessel for the control of ships moving in the western approaches of the Solent. While Bess prepared *Gossip* and struggled with the engine I rowed out to this splendid yacht and was politely ushered on board by a naval rating who took my painter and made it fast. As I climbed the smart companionway I was received by a petty officer who asked my business and when I said I required a permit to take a yacht to Cowes for repairs, I was taken before the Captain who asked me a number of questions, after which he issued me with an impressive document stating that I could sail the yacht *Gossip* to Cowes on September 3rd 1939.

Directly war was declared Bess and I tried to join up on active service and although she was trained in the First Aid Nursing Yeomanry (F.A.N.Y.) and I was a mobile Voluntary Aid Detachment (V.A.D.) it was months before we were called up. In the early days there was plenty to do at home and the black-out alone kept us busy for many working hours. All the young people were feeling the same, expecting to be off at once, but the paddle steamers to Lymington were crowded with visitors and Service people trying to leave the Island and we were asked to stay at home unless our business was essential. To keep our friends and ourselves active and occupied we started a bicycle polo team and every morning gangs of young people turned up at Norlands with bicycles and walking sticks, and worked off their energy charging up and down our tennis court. It was a great success and a reaction against the thought of war which was heavy on our minds.

I started work in the Air Raid Protection (A.R.P.) office almost at once and also spent two days a week at the Red Cross depot making 'many tails'. These objects were a type of bandage resembling a cat's cradle, as impossible to construct as a Chinese puzzle. They were difficult to cut out and even more difficult to put together. I don't know who used them, I certainly never saw one all the time I was in a naval hospital.

Work at the A.R.P. office was even worse and more frustrating because there was nothing to do and we sat hour after hour waiting for a raid which never came and only occasionally going out on exercises as it was considered a waste of petrol. We played racing-demon and rummy and told each other's fortunes in the tea leaves left at the bottom of our endless cups of tea. One hated duty was to clear up each morning after the A.R.P. cat, a mangy creature with nasty habits, called 'Orace. One man made such a fuss when it was his morning on 'cat duty' that we all played up to him. We arrived early one morning before he was due and made little models of 'Orace's messes in plasticine which we deposited in odd corners all over the sordid building. It was an enormous success, exceeding our greatest expectations. Cursing and swearing he armed himself with a shovel and bucket of sand and complaining bitterly of the smell carefully covered each little mound with sand before lifting it at arm's length with the shovel.

'Many tails' bandages and plasticine models were hardly my idea of war work and I longed for action. I was very glad when the manager of the yard at Cowes informed us late in November that he had repaired *Gossip*'s stern gland and we could collect her any day.

It was a bitterly cold day early in December when Bess and I took time off from our activities and armed with another permit and a volunteer crew, we took a bus into Cowes to take charge once more. One of the men at the yard took pleasure in informing us that their cat had given birth to kittens in our storm jib and that one of the progeny was named 'Chit Chat' out of *Gossip*. I hoped she had nicer habits than 'Orace, but years later Lucia reported nests of fleas living in comfort in this sail, which was very seldom used and it's possible they could have remained dormant or in a state of suspended animation tucked up in the sail locker.

Our sail back to Yarmouth stands out as being one of the coldest in living memory. We had to beat all the way in the teeth of a northwesterly wind. The engine stuttered and ground to a halt before we were out of the Medina River and the rain turned to sleet as we rounded Egypt Point and was difficult to distinguish from the icy spray which shot up over the bows in the race off Gurnard Ledge. We were cold and dejected by the time we reached Yarmouth and didn't relish the idea of sailing into the harbour with no engine in such wretched conditions, so we hailed *The Star of India* and after realizing our plight she provided a motor launch to tow us up to our moorings.

The cold winter dragged on but we were blest with a fine, warm early spring and Bess and I were suddenly inspired with the idea of fitting out *Anthea*. We worked on her in all our free time, doing all the work ourselves and on April 1st 1940, with all the help we could muster, we dragged her out of the Yarmouth One Design shed, towed her through Yarmouth Square in her ungainly cradle and launched her from the quay. We had already been granted a fishing permit - the only legitimate way of war-time sailing - and armed with this we sailed over to Lymington to meet Dambom who was due to come home that afternoon on twenty-four hours' leave. He was delighted to see us and sailed back to Yarmouth clad in full uniform with gas mask and tin hat at the ready and a mackerel line over the stern to show the naval patrols that we really were fishing.

Bess was called up by the F.A.N.Y. a few days later and I was told to stand by to join my Commandant, Miss Waistell, in Northern France, on twelve hours' notice. However, days went by and I never received any orders and having left the A.R.P. office I was free to sail whenever I liked.

Sailing alone is one of the most peaceful pursuits in the world. I learnt to love it in those weeks of spring and early summer and was out on my own most days, keeping well within the restricted areas marked on the chart. There was one prohibited area which stretched from a mark off Yarmouth Common eastwards as far as Bouldnor Fort, and there were instructions up on the Club board stating that 'all vessels were to keep clear of the area and if they found themselves drifting inadvertently in these waters they were to anchor'.

One lovely day towards the end of May I took *Anthea* out of the harbour and sailed over to Lymington. The wind dropped on my return and although I edged up all I could to the east, by the time I had crossed the Solent I was on the wrong side of the pier. The tide was flooding and taking me towards the prohibited area. The wind died completely. I knew I couldn't row her against the tide and I was only a hundred yards from the mark buoy, so following the instructions laid down on the Club notice-board, I faced the inevitable and threw my anchor over the bow. It was very deep in that area, 500 yards out from the pier, so I let out the full cable but the small C.Q.R. anchor showed no sign of holding. In a panic now I crawled into the fore-peak looking for more rope. I found a short-coil of hemp and bent it on, gradually easing it over the bow. Still it didn't hold and I was almost in the forbidden waters. Frantic by now I looked for more rope. Should I use the main sheet? It was a difficult decision. If the wind got up suddenly as it so often did in the Solent, it would be dangerous to have the anchor attached to the main sheet. I decided against it. Funny how fast one could move with the anchor down. It must be springs again. I worked out the tides and decided it was. I was in the fatal area now, the buoy swirled past me, or so it seemed, the white foam creaming round it. Oh well! I had done as I was told, there was nothing more I could do, probably it didn't matter anyway, just another senseless restriction. I sat on deck sunning myself, speculating how far I would drift before the tide turned, in two, no three hours' time. I was moving at about three knots, in another three hours I might be nine miles away. I might even be at Cowes. I was opposite Bouldnor Fort now and the anchor decided to take a hold. Rather a nasty spot to settle in, I decided, with the guns of the fort pointing straight at me. After all, there was a war on and I was in forbidden territory. I suppose they were entitled to open fire. Suddenly I remembered something. This was the day when Michael Creagh-Osborne was due to take over the command of the fort. He knew *Anthea* well and had often sailed in her. I could rely on him not to shoot. But had he arrived? When did one take over a command, the day one arrived or the following morning? It was all important to me. Luckily, no one seemed to have observed me. I hoped the handing-over ceremony was taking place even now and I could remain in obscurity. All seemed peaceful so I settled down to sun myself on the deck.

Just as I had dropped off into a pleasant torpor induced by the sun I was roused by a shout close at hand.

'Ahoy there! Get your anchor and come with us.'

A naval launch was alongside me before I was aware of it. The anchor had made up for its early failure and now had a firm grip in the Bouldnor clay.

'I can't move it,' I said. 'Could you give me a hand?'

One of the three sailors leapt on board and made short work of it. He coiled the ropes neatly, undoing the knots with expert fingers and then made fast a tow line to the launch.

'The Captain's in a terrible state,' he said. 'You didn't ought to have sailed over the minefield. Proper dangerous too.'

So that was it. Why had I been so dim. I never even thought of a minefield although it seemed obvious now.

'Well,' I said, on the defensive now. 'It can't be a very good minefield if I can drag my anchor the whole way across it and I'm still alive to tell the tale.'

They towed me ignominiously back to Yarmouth, while I took down the sails with the help of the naval rating and tidied up the boat. I was taken alongside the pier virtually under arrest and moored alongside the patrol ship. One of the crew brought me a huge mug of naval brew tea, a drink I was to become all too familiar with, and I gratefully sipped the hot sweet fruity beverage whilst the whole crew surveyed me and wondered what my fate would be.

There was great speculation going on at the Yacht Club also about my fate. Captain Merriman, the officer in charge of X.D.O. West, had decided to hold a tea-party there that afternoon and had shattered his guests by his ready flow of language when, right before his very eyes, he saw the little white yacht capering over his precious minefield.

'What won't I do to that son of a gun!' he shouted storming out on to the balcony.

Meanwhile someone had brought a telescope to bear on the object of his fury.

'You can't do anything,' his colleague replied. 'It's a girl.'

The steward's wife joined the onlookers and quickly identified me.

'One of Colonel Brent-Good's daughters,' she said. 'She don't mean no harm, brought up nice them girls were.'

'I don't care how b..... well brought up she was,' thundered the Captain, 'but she certainly isn't harmless.'

Eventually a very polite sailor came on board *Anthea* and said, 'Captain Merriman's compliments, ma'am, and would you kindly hand over your sailing permit.'

I was gratified by this civil treatment and as the permit was a month out of date in any case and no more permits were being granted or old ones renewed, I felt I had got away, not only with my life, but with a free month's sailing also. After this little escapade, *Anthea* ended her wartime sailing and sat out the remaining five years with her companions in the Y.O.D. shed.

The war was going desperately badly at this time. The Germans were close to Paris and I had received a wire telling me not to proceed to France. I was getting more and more dejected. Surely someone wanted me somewhere.

Then came my chance. Rumours were going round about the terrible plight of our men who were cut off and abandoned somewhere in northern France and boats, any boats, were urgently needed to help bring them home. I thought about *Gossip*. Her engine was in working order now. She wasn't exactly fast but she might possibly get a tow across the channel and then work as a ferry taking the men from the shallow water to the big ships. I knew desperately that I wanted to go. This was something I could do, something *Gossip* could do. Once I had made up my mind I couldn't wait. I hurried over to the Pier Hotel, now the naval headquarters of X.D.O. West. I asked to see Captain Merriman and was ushered into his presence without delay.

'I would like to volunteer to take my father's yacht *Gossip* to help with the evacuation of our men,' I said. 'He's coming home today and I'm sure he will agree and he might even be able to come himself, but if not I would like to have an engineer as I'm not much good with engines.'

I was rather nervous as I stood before the Captain, not at the thought of the enterprise which only filled me with excitement, but because this was the first time I had seen him since my mishap on the minefield, and so I spoke very quickly and incoherently and had to say it all over again before he realized what I was saying.

He seemed quite interested and asked me a number of questions. The great problem of course was *Gossip*'s slow speed and the long distance from the Needles to Dunkerque, which I realized would be my destination but I had anticipated this and requested a tow for the first stage of the enterprise. He wrote everything down and said he would get in touch with me immediately if I was required. Meanwhile, I said I would get permission from my father and lay in the necessary stores and he agreed to supply me with an engineer and petrol for the trip.

I was highly elated and collected my tin hat and sailing clothes and looked out some provisions. By the time Dambom came home at lunch time I was well organized. He regretted that he couldn't get leave to come but put no difficulties in my way. However, I was thwarted again. I stood by the telephone all that day and the next and then the news came through that the evacuation from Dunkerque, the greatest evacuation of all time, was completed. I was too late.

Bess had been called up by the F.A.N.Y. in April and in July I joined my Commandant as a V.A.D. at the Royal Naval Hospital, Haslar. Lucia joined the W.R.N.S. after she had finished her Domestic Science training at Eastbourne and Alan, who was at his preparatory school when war broke out, joined up as a Gunner shortly after his seventeenth birthday.

In July 1943 I was drafted to Yarmouth as V.A.D. in charge of the W.R.N.S. in that area. I had my own sick-bay in Norton Lodge, the house opposite Norlands with its grounds stretching down to the waters of the Solent, which was built by my great-great-grandfather in 1794. It now rejoiced in the name of H.M.S. *Manatee* (or Sea Cow) and was the combined operations base for landing craft.

My sick-bay looked out over the Solent and the following spring I was fascinated by the peculiar objects which were constantly drifting past my line of vision. One day it might be an enormous structure like a four-poster bed with its feet in the air. Another time great planks of wood followed by posts of every shape and size, trailing behind a small tug, and once I saw giant cotton reels swiftly moving out towards the Needles. What could it mean? What could they be?

The wooden structures I learnt afterwards were parts for the Mulberry harbour and the giant cotton reels were for 'Pluto', the pipeline under the ocean, invented by Bernard Ellis, an eminent member of the Royal Cruising Club.

The Solent was a wonderful sight at this time. Line upon line of ships stretched from Yarmouth to Hamstead and then a further similar formation from Salt Mead buoy to Cowes. All were inert, silent and waiting. I was one of the few lucky enough to move amongst this fleet as I often accompanied the Medical Officer in the M.F.V. which served as a water ambulance. A great number of the boats were American Liberty Ships and all personnel had been 'briefed' so if any sick had to be taken ashore, they came with labels attached saying they were not to be questioned and were on oath not to divulge any plans. This didn't stop the generous Americans from showering our boat with chocolate and cigarettes when we came alongside.

On June 5th 1944, the landing craft from H.M.S. *Manatee* started moving off. First went the heavy, ungainly landing craft kitchens. They left at two o'clock and were followed by the slow moving troop-carriers and maintenance craft from our base. All that long afternoon they moved out towards the Needles in a slow steady stream.

A film show was laid on in the big hall that evening to occupy those of us who were left behind but I couldn't just sit watching fictitious deeds when here. within a stone's throw of the house, history was being made and our own men from this very camp were making it. I crept out of the room with Ruth Kitson, a Wren petty officer and kindred spirit, and led her up to the top of the house beyond my sick-bay and through a secret passage which revealed a narrow flight of stairs leading straight out on to the roof. We stood on a small flat area which was covered with lead. I knew the place well and sometimes escaped there when I wanted to be alone. It was a beautiful still evening and we could hear the steady thrum of passing engines. A solid mass of shipping - probably the Liberty Ships - was moving.

Dimly we could discern the shapes in the half-light. On and on they went, hour after hour.

It was strange that I should be watching this wonderful invasion force from the house of my great-great-grandfather, the Admiral. He must have stood on this exact spot many times far back in the eighteenth century and seen many beautiful full-rigged ships; barques and brigs and barquentines, caravels and carracks, but had he ever seen an armada like this? Had he ever seen a whole fleet of ships passing in the night, a fleet which carried the hopes and prayers of the whole nation? I very much doubted it, I very much doubted if anything like this had ever been seen before.

Ruth and I stood together on the roof, with no thought of time. We prayed for the success of the enterprise and we had faith in our prayers.

1946 – The Great Scrub

Although V.J. Day was on August 15th 1945, I wasn't demobilized until March of the following year, when I arrived home from Colombo, where I had been serving as a V.A.D. in the Royal Naval Hospital, to find that Lucia had just become engaged to Desmond Dillon, a lieutenant in the Royal Marines.

Desmond had grown up in boats much as we had, having done his early sailing in Bosham Creek. He was the youngest of three boys and at a very early age he had to stand by and watch his brothers sailing their dinghy as he was still a non-swimmer and it was a family rule that no boy could go out in a boat until he could swim. Day after day he watched them and gradually his envy turned to fury and his fury gave him strength and determination. He decided to make his own arrangements. There was an old rubber tyre in the garage. He knew it would float because he had once seen one whirling round in an eddy in the harbour. He waited until the coast was clear, then tying a rope round the tyre he dragged it down the bank to the creek. Now all he needed was a sail. He knew just what he wanted. He hurried back to the

house and selected the largest umbrella from the
stand in the hall. It happened to be a gorgeous red
one. Now his arrangements were complete. He ran
back to the creek and climbing into the tyre he
pushed off from the bank into the deep water. He
opened his beautiful red umbrella and held it at the
right angle to catch the wind. It succeeded beyond
his wildest dreams and in an ecstasy of delight the
tiny fair-haired boy was carried down the creek into
forbidden waters and a future Olympic silver
medallist was launched on his maiden voyage.

After the tyre, which only enjoyed a very short life,
Desmond sailed the 'Gawallop', an old box fitted
with a home-made sail and then gradually up-graded
his craft until by the end of the war he owned and
raced a twelve-foot National dinghy. It seemed only
natural that Lucia and Desmond should plan to spend
their honeymoon on *Gossip*. Dambom was delighted
and readily gave his consent, but I don't think
anyone realized the mammoth task that lay ahead if
we were to have her ready for their wedding in July.

Before the war, *Gossip* was a yacht that might have
graced any harbour with her spotless white topsides,
her well-scrubbed teak decks and her golden spars
but when we dragged her out of her mud-berth in the
Yar River at the end of March that year she was
almost unrecognizable. The grey protective paint
with which we had covered her in 1940 blended with
the river mud so that the whole effect was of some
sexless sea-slug or slimy sea-hare. Even her decks
were covered with mud where the tarpaulin had been
torn aside and down below in the saloon and cabin
the paint was flaking off the bulkheads, the lovely
panelling was dank and lustreless and the looking-
lamps and loo-seat had been carried off by
marauders.

Fitting out each spring had always been done by
Dambom and, of course, 'the girls', and the only
outside help we ever had was for the 'Great Scrub',
an annual event, and for stepping the mast which was

done every third year. Naturally, nothing had happened to change this custom. We were a most conservative family and so, as soon as we had recovered from the shock of seeing our desolate yacht, we realized that most of the damage was only skin-deep and after towing her into the harbour (the engine having seized up) and mooring her alongside an immobile motor-yacht called *Zilla*, we looked out our scrubbers and scrapers and started work.

Up for 'The Great Scrub', Yarmouth quay

For the first few weeks there was very little to show for our efforts as we were simply removing the dirt, scrubbing the decks daily with good salt water and scraping and burning off the old paint and varnish. We decided to abandon all hope of painting her white again and settled on a shade of emerald-green for her topsides which was most successful in covering all traces of the battleship-grey.

With the better weather in May we were able to complete the painting and start on the varnishing but the sun seemed to open up hidden faults in the deck caulking and various leaks appeared in the saloon. Rows of little droplets fused together, forming runnels along the bulkhead before dripping on to the settees. This proved a real problem and eventually Dambom mixed a cloggy substance made from putty and sump-oil and Lucia and I, with great patience, worked it in between every plank on deck, stuffing it down to supplement the caulking and topping it with a sticky skin of 'Seelastik'. It was a tedious and boring job and we always welcomed any diversion. One morning a large herd of cattle were driven over the bridge, only a hundred yards from where we were moored. They were mostly Galloway steers which had wintered on the downs and were now being exported to the mainland but there was one Guernsey cow amongst them - probably by mistake - and as we watched, the poor beast, alarmed by the mounted cowboys and rough, pushing steers, broke away from the herd and, charging down the muddy slope, plunged into the harbour where she was soon carried out of her depth by the current. Lucia and I dropped our Seelastik and scrambled into the dinghy to rescue the poor animal. We had never come up alongside a cow before and found it very difficult as she was terrified of the oars and kept moving away from us. Eventually she caught her leg between the pylons under the bridge and we were able to clutch her by the horns and get the Painter round her neck. Gradually we pulled her ashore, towing her alongside the dinghy and, barefooted as we were, we manoeuvred her along the main road and put her into our field to recover from her swim.

Gossip's spars were stored at the end of every sailing season in the old stables at Norlands where Dambom used to work on them in the winter, scraping and re-varnishing them so that they were all ready to be put on board when the time was ripe. This may sound a simple operation and without the mast it wasn't too bad, but this year we had everything.

Dambom, aided by Bess, Lucia and me, started with the long heavy boom which we lifted on to the small trolley - a primitive affair consisting of two small iron wheels supporting a block of wood - then all bending low in a back-breaking position in order to reach the spar we trundled it down the bumpy gas-work's lane, across the main road and down the Admiral's steps into the creek. The other spars, consisting of the bowsprit, topsail yards and spinnaker boom, followed in the same way, after which they were all attached to the stern of the dinghy which Dambom rowed down the creek to the harbour, the medley of spars trailing in his wake. We three then walked down to the sand-house (now converted into a boatyard) and were picked up in the dinghy by Dambom after he had attached his 'tow' to *Gossip*. We then went on board and with a series of pulleys hoisted the spars on deck.

The mast had its own launching drill. We had to mount it on two trolleys, the little low one used for the boom and an extra one made from some old pram wheels rescued from the 'dump'. After manipulating it through the stable gate, never an easy job with the cross-trees a vulnerable hazard, we dragged it on its uneven carriage down the lane and along the main road the whole way to the sand-house. It was far too long and awkward to take through the yard, so we had to roll it off its trolleys and with the aid of four rope slings, drag it to the quay-side and lower it carefully into the water. From there it only had a short sea voyage trailing behind Dambom in the dinghy to reach the jetty, from where it was lifted out of the water by the crane and poised ready for delivery. *Gossip*, meanwhile, was brought alongside and, mercifully, Tom Kelloway and Harold Hayles were always there to help us with the actual stepping.

When it was too cold or wet to work on deck we worked below and gradually the saloon, cabin and fo'c's'le became habitable and clean once more. We gave up all hope of bringing back a shine to the panelling, but made quite a good job of it by rubbing it down with sand-paper and applying two coats of varnish. We painted all the ceilings white, lying on our backs with the paint dripping on our faces and all the doors and woodwork, which had been polished before the war, we treated with varnish like the panelling and it had the advantage of saving a lot of work in the future.

In spite of the bad weather that year most of the painting, rigging and deck work was completed by the middle of June and at high-water springs at the end of the month we took her alongside the quay and prepared for the 'Great Scrub'.

Most of the work on board could be done in our own time and in selected weather conditions, but the scrubbing-berth had to be booked in advance as only one yacht could lie alongside at a time and she would only dry out completely at dead low water during the spring tides. This made us entirely dependent on the moon so regardless of wind, rain and foul weather, the scrub always took place on the appointed day and we had to work really hard to complete the job between the tides.

After mooring *Gossip* alongside the quay we had to get out all the fenders and the heavy wooden 'distance block' to keep her from lying directly against the wall and then we fastened pulleys from the mast-head to the quay to ensure her listing properly. This had to be completed by noon, then leaving Dambom on board to see that she took the ground correctly, we would collect all the old scrubbing brushes, paint brushes, rags and tins of antifouling paint from Norlands and bring them to the scene of action. Lunch was eaten on board or sitting on the quay and by two o'clock when the tide was falling, we would all appear in our special antifouling outfits.

This year, after the war, I appeared in dungarees with F.P. in large red letters on the bib - a relic of my 'fire patrol' outfit for fighting incendiaries at Haslar - rubber boots, sou'wester and large yellow Mickey-Mouse style rubber gloves. Bess wore her A.T.S. working overalls and tied her hair up in a bright green scarf and Lucia turned up looking like an

escaped convict in Alan's army trousers, her old
Wren top and a bath cap.

This was one of the rare occasions when help was
allowed. Our faithful gardener, Sid, who came to
Norlands in 1914 and produced wonderful vegetables
out of the solid unrelenting clay soil for over forty
years, never missed a scrub. Our other helper was
Murrow, who looked after the house and family with
love and devotion for over thirty years. These
excellent workers always turned up with great good
humour, in their own version of anti-fouling outfits,
directly the scrubbing started.

First we had to brush off all the accumulated weed,
starting as soon as the tide left any part uncovered.
This had to be done from the dinghy with two people
holding the painters on deck and two scrubbing
frantically from the dinghy. Gradually, as the water
receded it was possible to stand on the bottom in
rubber boots and then we worked like maniacs all
scrubbing at once with any brush, long or short,
which we could lay hands on. Lower down on the
hull there were hard encrusted barnacles which could
only be removed with a knife or a scraper, and most
revolting of all, were the slimy red sea-squirts which
had to be scraped off in a similar way, but they fell
all round our feet and were sluggish, creepy and
repulsive.

'Yea slimy things did crawl with legs upon a slimy
sea.'

Actually they were legless beasties but they seemed
to move on the water with the motion of the waves,
squelching and squirting from their twin siphons.

As soon as a large area had been scrubbed it was
wiped down with a bundle of old rags and one of us
would then start slapping on the anti-fouling. This
was thick sludgy paint, stiff and cloggy to put on.
Sometimes we used ordinary paint brushes and
sometimes rollers plunged in meat tins of red paint.

Either way it was hard work. Bess prided herself on painting the water-line, so this was always her job and we all walked about on the bottom of the sea scrubbing, scraping and painting in frantic haste to complete the job before the impatient water moved in again. There was only a very short time when we could really reach the bottom of the hull and it was inevitable that we painted in layers, one holding a tin above the other, so that head protection from dripping paint was essential.

As the tide came up the sea around us was blood-red with brush droppings and we must have looked a 'ghastly crew' in our weird outfits with pale, exhausted faces, hurrying, ever hurrying with brushfuls of dripping red paint. High above us on the quay, the inhabitants of Yarmouth and an interested gathering of 'trippers' would watch our progress and utter comments in loud unguarded voices, probably in ignorance of the fact that we were even partly human.

Gossip always seemed enormous when she lay dried out and naked by the quay and it really was a large area of hull to cover against time but at last it would be finished and we would be able to relax and enjoy surveying our work and each other's paint-smeared faces.

This was by no means the end of the day. Someone, usually Dambom, had to stay on board to see that she took the water safely when the tide came in then, twelve hours after we had brought her alongside, came 'Midnight Manoeuvres'.

This entailed turning out again, invariably in the wind and rain, in pitch darkness to take the yacht back to her berth at the far end of the harbour. The year 1946 was no exception. Just before midnight we drove down to the quay in teeming rain and boarded *Gossip* who was afloat once more. After casting off the warps by the aid of a single torch, Dambom started towing from the dinghy as, needless to say, the engine was out of action. It was hardly our fault that the wind caught the yacht just as we turned up the main channel and swept her against a smart motor-cruiser. Bess was steering and Lucia and I rushed forward with fenders, but we were too late to avoid a nasty crunch as the ships closed together and a human form suddenly loomed up alongside and yelled something we scarcely understood! Dambom, realizing something was up but conveniently deaf, rowed all the harder and, as Lucia and I pushed off, we slid away stealthily into the welcome darkness of the night.

By the time we were finally moored alongside *Zilla* and had made our way ashore and reclaimed the car it was one o'clock but the 'Great Scrub' was over for another year.

Although Dambom never ordered us to turn up for this annual event, it became a point of honour with the three of us all through our lives that we should be there when the great day came. I remember Bess coming back from Paris one year especially for the occasion. She arrived off the Lymington ferry early one morning when we were preparing to bring *Gossip* alongside. Lucia and I gazed at her in astonishment as she stood on the quay, ready to receive our warps, dressed in a stylish suit and gay Parisian hat.

'Whatever are you doing?' I said. 'We didn't expect you back for another week.'

'I came for the Scrub of course,' said Bess. 'Remember, I always do the water-line.'

In later years Lucia and I considered pregnancy gave exemption but no other excuse ever satisfied our self-enforced code of honour.

Lucia and Desmond were married on the only really nice day we had all that cold wet summer.

Desmond probably found our family a little unusual. He had expected Dambom to take him aside and have a father-in-lawly talk with him at some time during the engagement. Nothing happened however, until the entire family were gathered in the vestry to sign the register after the marriage service. At that solemn moment Dambom beckoned to Desmond who went up to him in some apprehension.

'By the way, my boy,' said Dambom. 'There's something I ought to tell you. It came to me during the service. I shackled on the anchor outside the bowsprit shrouds by mistake. You must clear it as soon as you get on board.'

Lucia wore her 'going away' dress from Norlands to the Royal Solent Yacht Club, a distance of half a mile, and then changed into red slacks before she and her husband rowed out to their honeymoon ship.

Meanwhile, Tom Kelloway, aided and abetted by Harold Hayles, had not been idle. He had decorated the lovely old sandhouse with a variety of flags, probably borrowed from all the yachts in the harbour and after continuing the theme all along the jetty, he set to work on *Gossip*.

When Lucia and Desmond went on board they were confronted with bunches of roses on the bowsprit and anchor chain, a spray of greenery below the Royal Naval Sailing Association burgee at the mast-head and two large and inelegant boots firmly lashed to the cross-trees. Quite undaunted Desmond started the engine. Miracle of miracles it worked and they motored out of the harbour to the cacophony of fog horns, sirens and cheers.

When they were out in the Solent and well clear of Yarmouth they were surprised to hear a strange variety of hoots issuing from a passing Polish liner who was obviously trying to attract their attention. Realizing something was amiss they looked around the yacht and only then did they see, written across their starboard bow in large white letters the words 'WE ARE JUST MARRIED'. Tom Kelloway and his merry men had certainly been thorough.

They spent the first night quietly anchored in Totland Bay but that was the end of the one-day summer. The next morning they sailed past the

coloured sands of Alum Bay and out of the Needles
channel bound for Weymouth but once clear of the
Solent they were confronted by a very lumpy sea
which had been knocked up by the strong south-
westerly wind. An hour later, in a freshening wind,
Lucia went forward to reef the mainsail and, for the
first time in her life, was sea-sick. Clutching the fore-
hatch she lay down on the deck and let the waves
break over her. Desmond, who was steering at the
time, looked forward and found she had vanished.
One minute she was there, standing by the mast,
vivid and vital in her red oilskins and seconds later,
when he looked again, there was no sign of her, only
the waves breaking over the bow and surging along
the deck. Terrified that he had lost his bride, he left
the helm and made his way forward where he found
her limp and prostrate on deck. Carefully he brought
her back to the cockpit and resuming the helm, he
turned the yacht round and headed for the Needles.

They spent the remainder of their honeymoon,
during that summer of wind and rain, moving from
port to port in the sheltered waters of the Solent.

Their first child was born just a year later. There
was a Y.O.D. series race in progress at the crucial
moment. Desmond had been persuaded to race
Katinka for Geraldine Cross and Bess and I were in
Anthea, but although it was a race of some
importance, every time we came in sight of Norlands
we cast covert glances at the bare white flagstaff on
the lawn, hoping to see the signal which Dambom
had promised to send us as soon as Lucia's baby was
born. When we were tacking along inshore close to
the sand-spit on the second round, Desmond 'called
for water'. We tacked once more, complying with the
racing rules and *Katinka* tacked and came up on our
weather. The same instant Bess shouted, 'Watch the
flagstaff.' For the moment the race was forgotten and
all eyes watched as the flags crept up the naked

▲
Dambom aged five

▶
Cecily and Jay on
the river Yar in *Tigger*

◀ *Gossip* at Berg on the Göta
Canal. Bess (left) and
Cecily (right

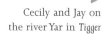

▶
Jay (Lucia), Cecily
and Dambom on
Mount Vesuvius

The author in 2002, in the Royal Solent Yacht Club. The model of *Gossip* was made for Dambom by Cecily's cousin, Ronald Saxby.

mask. First came the Union Jack and then the all important second flag. Was it international code 'B, (denoting a boy in Brent-Good code) or the blue and yellow striped 'G' (denoting a girl)? As we watched the broad pennant red flag 'B' climbed slowly up the mast, followed by all the flags in 'dress formation' proclaiming to the Y.O.D. class in particular and to the watchers in Yarmouth in general, that Dambom's first grandson, Graeme, had arrived.

1947-48 – Holland Re-visited

In 1947 *Gossip* ceased to be the centre of attraction as a glamorous honeymoon ship and after the normal re-fit Dambom, Ronald and I set out on our first post-war cruise with Holland as our objective.

Desmond accompanied us as far as the Royal Marine Barracks at Eastney and after our prearranged signal had been observed, his batman rowed out to us as we lay 'hove to' and took him ashore.

We spent the first night at Bosham and the following morning cleared the bar at Chichester harbour determined to make Dover our next port of call. It was a quiet peaceful day but the light winds were everywhere and we were kept busy changing the sails. We rounded Beachy Head just before dark in the softest of southerly winds and set our next course to pass outside the Royal Sovereign light vessel. We shared the watches of the night but made little progress as the light breeze scarcely moved us against the tide and when dawn broke we found ourselves off Hastings.

I was on watch at half past six that morning when Dambom came on deck to check our position. Ronald, waking at the same time, decided we were all in need of breakfast and soon an encouraging aroma of bacon and eggs and coffee wafted astern making me realize how hungry I was. Dambom, attracted by the smell, turned to go below, leaving me in a state of happy torpor at the helm. Fortunately just before he disappeared down the hatchway he looked astern. In a second he was on deck again, instantly alert.

'It can't be,' he muttered. 'I've only seen it once before and never m this country, but, by God, if it is ... Ronald!' he shouted, 'Come on deck.'

Already he was lowering the balloon foresail and rolling up the jib. Ronald, abandoning the half-cooked breakfast, shot up through the fore-hatch to his side. Together they started reefing the mainsail. Then it hit us.

A great surge of wind rushed up astern, roaring and bellowing like the stampede of a thousand angry bulls. I never looked aft. I was concentrating on the steering with every sense alert and every muscle tensed and so I never saw it. I never saw the hard black line across the sky which Dambom had rightly interpreted as a 'line squall'.

The men were rolling in the reefs as fast as they could. Luckily nothing went wrong. I knew by instinct that I had to keep the yacht dead before the wind. If I gybed in that force of wind nothing could save the mast or the two men who were wrestling with the reefing-gear and if I let her come into the wind, even for a second, I would lose control and she would 'broach to' which would probably mean the loss of the ship.

Cutting the hoops from the mast Dambom rolled in the reefs as Ronald lowered the sail until the claws of the gaff were right down to the foot of the mast. This rapid roller-reefing made a far more efficient job than lowering the sail altogether, when it would have been almost impossible to tie it down effectively in that sudden weight of wind. It also had the advantage of keeping the yacht under control and the tiny peak of sail which remained seemed to steady her and drive her before the wind like a Flying Dutchman planing on the surface. The whole sky darkened as the tornado - for such I believe it was - swept overhead and hissed and thundered eastwards towards Dungeness.

Seven minutes it lasted, from the moment Ronald came on deck until the last roll had been put in the mainsail. Then the light came back into the sky. The wind dropped from the west as suddenly as it had risen and the gentle southerly breeze returned as though nothing had happened. *Gossip* drifted on the ruffled sea, her tiny sail an insult to the friendly wind but she was safe and thanks to Dambom's backward glance before the squall hit us, so were we. Ronald, unperturbed and eminently practical, served breakfast as usual.

Our entry to Dover harbour was nearly a disaster. I was steering for the south entrance when Dambom remarked, 'Something odd there, I'd better check it in *Reed's Almanac*.'

The 'odd' thing turned out to be the masts and funnel of a sunken ship lodged in the fairway, as confirmed by *Reed's*.

After making a successful entry by the eastern passage we decided to go straight into the Granville dock where we could lie quietly alongside instead of rolling about in the open harbour.

It was as well we did. The glass dropped throughout the day and by nightfall there was a full gale. Altogether we spent four nights in the dock waiting for the gale to abate. Finally, after a morning of solid rain, the conditions looked more hopeful and as the forecast that evening promised us a westerly wind Force 5, we planned to leave early the next morning.

It was still dark when the dock opened at half past three so we tied up to a lamp-post on the quay to await the dawn.

'Ere, you can't do that!' shouted someone out of the darkness, and a large policeman appeared from nowhere sweeping *Gossip* with the beam of his powerful torch.

'Can't do what?' asked Dambom.

'Why, tie yer boat up to that there lamp-post,' he said. 'You might pull it over. Besides, it's against regulations.'

If it hadn't been quite so early in the morning, we might have laughed at the idea of *Gossip* heaving out lamp-posts, as it was, we moved further down the quay, quietly submissive.

When dawn broke, about two hours later, we slipped out of the harbour and set a course for Calais. The wind was south-westerly, about Force 4, when we left but it gradually increased all through the day and *Gossip* sped before it. I think this was the most exciting and spectacular sail she ever accomplished. None of us wanted to go into Calais, so in spite of the strong wind, we altered course for Dunkerque.

After passing the Dyck buoy off Gravelines, we referred to our special post-war chart which showed all the wrecked ships with their own particular buoys and marked all the minefields, some of which it stated might 'still remain active'.

Every hour the wind increased and every hour the two men rolled in another reef until we were surging ahead at our maximum speed of seven knots, with seven rolls in the mainsail which was reefed down to the last two hoops on the mast. Ronald and I were exhilarated and felt we never wanted to stop. Occasionally I cast a furtive look astern from my place at the wheel. The seas were thundering up behind thrusting us forward, but *Gossip* always seemed to ride on the crest of the waves without sinking into the troughs and her counter stern gave her such buoyancy aft that the following seas never harmed her or endangered her in any way.

Dambom looked worried at times and when Ronald and I were hungrily awaiting lunch he stood transfixed in the gangway unconsciously opening a tin of meat with his thoughts far away on the rising wind. After five minutes' contemplation he handed Ronald the tin which was so badly opened that he had to gouge the contents out of the jagged rat-hole before we could appease our hunger.

Eleven hours after leaving Dover we literally surged up Ostend harbour, came into the wind and dropped our anchor off the Yacht Club where the storm cone was suspended from the flagstaff. Some of the members rowed out and offered us hospitality, impressed by our spectacular entry but they were incredulous when they heard we had come from England as they had been sitting tight all day listening to the gale which registered Force 8 on the Beaufort scale.

We spent a day stormbound in Ostend enjoying the rich food which we hadn't tasted since before the war and loading the ship with such luxuries as sweets, chocolates, cakes, cigarettes and cream which we could buy without restriction in this land of plenty. The delicious sole we had for dinner the night we arrived, after our memorable sail, were swimming in butter and the gateau which followed was a symphony of cream and chocolate.

It was lucky we feasted whilst we were in Belgium, for when we reached Flushing, we found ourselves once more in a country of food rationing. I went ashore before breakfast on our first morning in Holland and seeing several men on the quay I asked where I could buy bread and milk.

'Have you a ration-card?' they asked. 'You can't buy anything now without a card.'

When I explained that we had sailed over from England they told me that I was entitled to cards but couldn't obtain them until the office opened at ten o'clock.

As it was still very early and I didn't intend hanging about for two hours, I turned back to the dinghy, but one of the men came after me.

'Give me your milk-can,' he said, 'and follow me.'

Meekly, I followed as he wove in and out of the cobbled streets. Presently he told me to wait and he disappeared inside a house. After a few minutes he emerged with a full can and then continued walking through the town. Again he disappeared, motioning me to wait outside and this time he appeared carrying a loaf of bread, fresh and warm from the bakery and a wicker-basket full of large brown eggs. When he had escorted me back to the quay he handed me his purchases.

'Thank you very much,' I said. 'Please tell me what I owe you?' 'You owe me nothing,' he replied. 'You were plenty good to us in the war and I am very pleased to help you.'

I was very touched by this reply but was even more impressed by his generosity when we went ashore after breakfast and I saw the acres and acres of good farming land now lying waste because we had been forced to bomb the dykes and flood the land during the German occupation. It would be five or six years before they could grow crops again on the salt-encrusted soil but they understood our reasons for causing this devastation and blessed us for saving their country.

After obtaining our precious ration-cards, we left Flushing and entered the busy Wester Schelde River. We followed in the wake of the gaily painted barges to Hansweert, continuing the next day through the canals to Dordrecht and the active port of Rotterdam and on to ancient Delft where we tied up for the night.

Ronald had to leave us there as his leave was up and Sir Basil Gould, known always as B.J., took his place on *Gossip*.

B.J., who was to become my husband the following year, had just retired from the Indian Political Service. He started his apprenticeship in sail as owner of the six-metre *Polly*, which, with Alf Diaper as skipper, was the most successful yacht in the team which won the Seawanhaka Cup for Britain in 1921.

After he joined us at Delft we left *Gossip* lying alongside the wharf and went to The Hague for the day. First we went to my favourite art gallery the Mauritshuis, where B.J. presented me with a print of Potter's 'Young Bull', the picture I had been so taken with on my previous visit, and we wandered at leisure in this small but exquisite gallery amongst the Rembrandts and Vermeers, the Holbeins and the Hals. After lunch we visited the Peace Palace and sat in the restful rose garden before returning to Delft, the city immortalized by Vermeer.

From Delft we continued weaving our way through the canals to Amsterdam. Our progress was slow due to the numerous road and rail bridges which had to open to let us through. The smaller road bridges opened specially for us and the keeper exacted his fee by lowering a little coloured sabot on a long chain and holding it directly over the boat so that we could drop the appropriate coin into it as we passed through. We often added a cigarette or two and this always produced a smile and a profusion of thanks, but towards the end of the day we found we had run out of all our small change and when we tried to pay the full fee in the equivalent of cigarettes it was not too well received although they allowed us to pass.

We spent a whole day seeing the sights of the beautiful watery city of Amsterdam, leaving *Gossip* lying in the new yacht-haven and crossing the main harbour in the free ferry.

When we left the next morning the Secretary of the Yacht Club lowered the Union jack which had been flying since our arrival and dipped the Dutch flag in salute. This little act of courtesy, which they accord to all foreign yachtsmen, gave us great pleasure and we were quick to dip our ensign in response.

We sailed into the Zuider Zee that day and found many major alterations since our previous visit in 1933. The Dutch, who lead the world in land reclamation, had thrown a mighty dam across the entrance of this inland sea and reclaimed vast areas of land which were now cultivated and inhabited. The most interesting place we visited was Urk. This had been an island when we were there before. Now it was part of the mainland and I felt the inhabitants resented this and would rather be back in their former insular state.

The people of Urk are as unlike the Dutch as the Orcadians and Shetlanders are to the British. I went ashore in the early morning for milk, leaving the men to cook breakfast, but I soon wished I had a male escort as I sensed the hostility around me. I carried the milk-can through the cobbled streets and although I felt all eyes were on me, no one offered to help. The people of Urk have a magnificent physique. The women are large and very tall with exceptionally powerful arms and cold unsmiling faces and I felt they could have picked me up as though I was a Lilliputian and put me back in my dinghy. The men are tall and muscular and they gazed at me with cold steely-blue eyes, full of hostility. Somehow I managed to buy some milk at a tiny shop before hurrying back to *Gossip* and the protection of the men. I believe the citizens of Urk owe their great size and strength to their diet of eels, and I heard afterwards from a Dutch girl, that although they dislike all strangers, a woman in trousers, as I was, is their greatest bugbear.

From hostile Urk we sailed to Enkhuizen where we joined a number of yachtsmen on a rally from Amsterdam. They recognized *Gossip* from her sojourn in their yacht-haven and were all very friendly, inviting us on board their boats where everyone spoke excellent English and entertained us most lavishly.

A few days later we left the Zuider Zee Passing through the great lock-gates into the North Sea. We spent one night at Den Helder and then returned to Amsterdam.

It was now time to end our cruise and take *Gossip* to a yard near Amsterdam where we had already made arrangements for laying her up. The night before we reached the yard we found our way barred by a railway-bridge which only opened at fixed times, the next time being at six o'clock in the morning, so we anchored nearby and rose early so that we wouldn't miss this rare opportunity.

When the hour came we dressed hurriedly and as I came on deck I heard a faint 'plop' in the water followed by a shout from B.J.

'Damn! There goes my bottom set!'

In the upheaval of getting under way in time for the opening bridge we couldn't do anything about the lost teeth, but while Dambom struggled with the engine, B.J. and I managed to buoy the spot with a small cork fender floating above a heavy stone which I retrieved from the river bank when Dambom was busy below. The engine didn't start at all that day and so B.J. towed *Gossip* from the dinghy through the bridge and across to the yard.

Later in the day while Dambom was organizing the laying-up procedure, B.J. and I, armed with a grapnel, which I had adapted with a canvas sheath, set off in the dinghy to find our cork float. We spent an hour anchored over the spot dredging the area and retrieved all sorts of stones, shells and tins and even a handsome piece of Delft china, but as Mr. Jackson said to Mrs. Tittlemouse,

'No teeth, no teeth, no teeth'.

The following year Dambom, B.J. and John Roome, who was soon to become so well known in the R.O.R.C., went out to Holland to bring *Gossip* home

again. Unfortunately B.J. suffered from his old
enemy, the duodenal ulcer, during the cruise and
although John strained all his food, with infinite
patience, through a Red Ensign retrieved from the
sail-locker, it didn't improve matters and so after
asking Dambom for my hand in marriage he returned
to Yarmouth.

Dambom and John finished the cruise on their own
but were held up by headwinds so that they had only
reached Dover by the time my engagement was
reported in *The Times*. John, seeing the notice,
handed it to Dambom.

'Good Lord,' he said, slapping his sides with
laughter. 'Cecily Audrey - I never knew her name
was Audrey!'

B.J. and I were married that September in the old
church at Freshwater above the River Yar, and our
reception was held at Norlands on just such a perfect
day as Lucia and Desmond had had two years before.

James, our son, was born on November 5th 1949, in
our rambling old house overlooking the square.
Yarmouth is a peaceful town in winter and the
inhabitants are apt to hibernate for weeks on end but
on Guy Fawkes day they emerge like squirrels
searching for nuts and after the 'Guys' have been
judged by the Carnival Committee and darkness
falls, the square lights up in a weird medieval beauty
as hundreds of flaming torches are carried from the
old Town Hall by the citizens of Yarmouth, young
and old, who parade round the town with their
beacons held high above their heads. So it was on the
birthday of Dambom's second grandson, who lay in
his cot by my bedroom window as the flickering
lights moved past the house and the odd firework
flashed and crackled in the street below.

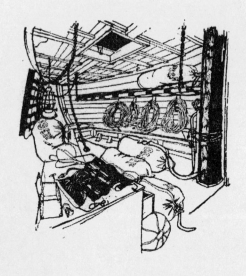

1952 – Houseboat

Gossip was usually away on her annual cruise from early June until late July and during August she would remain in the harbour, enjoying a Sabbatical month, while we raced *Anthea* at Cowes, Yarmouth and Lymington in the intensive Y.O.D. class programme. She would emerge again in September for short cruises, day sails and the Royal Cruising Club meet in the Beaulieu River which marked the end of the season.

Lucia was quick to see the advantage of this lull and when Desmond was away fighting in Korea in 1952 she let her house for the month of August and took over *Gossip* as a houseboat for herself, her two children – Graeme aged five and Susan three – and an attractive girl who was expected to act as a cross between a nanny and a bo'sun's mate.

Engaging the 'nanny' for the month's holiday was, of course, of the greatest importance. The first year Lucia selected a girl called Ann from a number of applicants who applied for the job, but it wasn't until they were going on board the first evening that she realised she had forgotten to ask her future employee if she could row. Unfortunately, it transpired that she had never been in a boat before which was a grave disadvantage as Lucia had planned to race every day, leaving her 'nanny' to ferry the children backwards and forwards to the beach or the landing stage in the dinghy.

Ann was an intelligent girl and next morning she was determined to teach herself this all important accomplishment, so giving the children an absorbing occupation down below, she came on deck and sat quietly in the cockpit studying form. There were all sorts of dinghies rowing round the harbour, it looked easy enough. Just then Mr. Doe rowed sedately by and Ann decided to emulate him. Surely his method must be the best, after all he was the Harbour Master and an important person as Graeme had already explained to her. Preparing for action she tied a long rope to the dinghy's painter and attaching it to *Gossip*'s stern she got into the dinghy and practised rowing it backwards and forwards on its long painter. By the time Lucia had returned from her first days racing Ann had achieved a good command of the boat, but her style was unusual as she sat facing the bow and rowing backwards! This happened to be a method peculiar to Mr. Doe who found it easier to see where he was going, as of course it was, when he went his rounds of the yachts collecting harbour dues.

The month passed without any major disasters and from then on *Gossip* was transformed into a houseboat every August.

It was a wonderful life for the Dillon children and for their cousin James, who was part of their life and shared all their hopes and fears. Dambom's grandchildren were at home in any sort of boat and very soon they were able to teach their own nannies to row. They wallowed in the succulent harbour mud at low water like young eels and washed themselves

in the clean water from the creek when the tide came
in before drying off in the sun on the sandy beach at
the western end of the sand-spit.

They learnt to swim early in life which was a great
relief to their harassed mothers. We made a rule that
they should always wear life-jackets on board until
they could satisfy Desmond that they could swim out
of their depths from the yacht *Zilla* to the sand-house
jetty, a distance of twenty yards. We named this the
'Zilla Test' and they practised for it all one summer.
They could easily cover the distance but didn't like
swimming over the great unknown where they
couldn't feel the bottom with their toes. James, the
youngest of the three and the weakest swimmer, was
the first to pass his test, but within a week the Dillons
followed suit and all three received certificates from
Desmond stating that they had passed the 'Zilla Test'
and were exempt from wearing their life-jackets in
the harbour.

Gossip certainly changed her character during these
houseboat sessions. By day she formed a happy
crèche for the children, but at night she took on quite
another character when poker parties replaced the
games of ludo and beggar-my-neighbour! As soon as
supper had been eaten and cleared away, Graeme and
Susan were sent to their bunks in the after-cabin, and
being true Dillons they fell asleep at once remaining
in a state bordering on coma for a good twelve hours,
regardless of the world around them. This was just as
well as we certainly had some riotous parties. The
saloon seemed very cosy when we were all gathered
round the table but just when we were settling down,
ready for play to commence, Lucia would decide to
light the 'Lord's Lamp' — a Tilly lamp given to
Dambom by a noble lord who crewed for him at one
time. Lighting it was a terrifying performance and I
always insisted on extricating myself from the saloon
and going on deck whilst the operation was in
progress. It was designed on the lines of a primus
stove and was set in action by igniting a bowl of

methylated spirits round the base. Hectic pumping followed and either it went out altogether, when the performance had to be repeated, or it belched forth lethal orange flames and clouds of thick black smoke and had to be held in the open hatch-way until it had settled down. When it was working it certainly gave an excellent light but halfway through the evening it was apt to fail and then we had to hold everything and clear the cards off the table while Lucia re-pumped it.

Sometimes when all the ship's money had been gambled away at poker we held sing-songs on board and sometimes we played that wild fanatical game racing-demon.

Coming on board in the evening and returning late at night in the dark was often a hazardous undertaking. The sand-house was locked at night and we had to use the 'soldiers' slip', a small landing stage which had been built for the R.A.S.C. during the war. It was situated opposite the Harbour Master's house on the bridge road and was always cluttered up by a fleet of small boats. At low water the wooden stage was so slippery with its coating of green slime that there were many accidents. One evening an eminent architect set out to join the party on *Gossip* and slipped as he was about to reach for the dinghy. He plunged into the water and disappeared in the blackness of the night. As he was unable to swim this caused a certain amount of consternation but his plaintive gurgles were detected by two fellow guests who pulled him to safety. It was unfortunate that he had just dined in Yarmouth and was resplendent in evening dress and patent leather pumps. Salt water is no respecter of clothes and his dinner jacket never regained its former suavity.

Pets had their place on the houseboat, or rather they were supposed to, but one of Susan's white mice had a 'happy event' on board and was improvident enough to produce eleven little ones, who within a very short time were running in and out of their cage through the bars which were too far apart to restrain them. This led to constant trouble and Susan was always burrowing round the ship searching for her little flock when they failed to turn up at feeding time. One evening I was walking over the bridge and as I looked down on the boats I saw the unusual sight of a large man crawling along the deck of a handsome blue yacht which was moored alongside *Gossip*. His portly posterior was directly in my line of vision, so that I was unable to see what he was doing, but suddenly he lunged forward and called out:

'Got you, you little devil!' and as he turned round Susan rushed up on deck and I saw him hand her something which I guessed rightly was one of her mice. Apparently they had become more venturesome and the owner of the blue yacht had been sitting quietly on deck enjoying his gin and tonic when suddenly he saw a dainty white mouse, her whiskers twitching, tripping elegantly along the warp and impudently boarding his ship.

After this incident Susan realized the mice were beyond her control and with hardly a pang she took them ashore and sold them for threepence apiece at the local pet shop. With the proceeds, she bought a golden hamster.

Rufous, as she named her new pet, settled down quite happily as the newest member of the crew and for a few days all was well, but Lucia woke up one night and heard a crunchy, gnawing noise which seemed to be coming from the bowels of the ship. Switching on her torch she went into the fo'c's'le and was confronted with an empty cage and no trace of the hamster. Presently the gnawing started again but still she couldn't find the miscreant. Sarah, the current 'nanny', now woke up and joined in the search. Working methodically through all the lockers in the fo'c's'le by torchlight they eventually found a small hole deep down behind the paraffin tins. Frantic now, they turned out the locker. No Rufous.

The ominous gnawing sound continued. It was quite obvious that the industrious little rodent was in the cavity between the locker wall and the ship's planking and, judging by the noise, he was working overtime to abandon ship. They couldn't tell if he was working above or below the water line, in either case it looked as if a nasty situation was about to develop. Lucia routed through the tool box looking for a saw; she planned to enlarge the hole in the locker and remove the animal before he made a hole in the ship's side, but Sarah, the level-headed daughter of the Commandant-General of the Royal Marines, decided to try strategy rather than force. She produced a fresh, succulent carrot from the vegetable locker and held it near the scene of action. The gnawing ceased and soon greedy Master Rufous popped his little red head through the hole. He remained hesitantly in that position for a few seconds, blinking his wicked little eyes in the torchlight, while the watchers waited with bated breath and then deciding that it looked a tolerably good carrot and would probably taste better than seasoned teak, he pushed his fat little body through the hole and allowed himself to be recaptured.

In addition to the hole in the paraffin locker and the persistent smell of white mice which lurked in odd corners of the ship, the Dillons left behind as evidence of their occupation a number of little paper golliwogs which gradually formed a freize round the fo'c's'le wall and grew in length and variety every year as the young Dillons ate their way through pot after pot of Golden Shred marmalade and strawberry jam.

1953 – Brittany

Gossip reviewed the Fleet at Spithead on June 13th 1953, following the Coronation of Queen Elizabeth II. She carried a ship's complement of twelve and we had to serve lunch in relays to feed them all. There was standing room only on deck but as she sailed close to the line of ships everyone had a front line view.

Four days later, with Dambom, Bess and Philip Cheverton, one of Alan's school friends on board, she turned her long bowsprit once more towards her favourite sailing grounds of Brittany.

Dambom had been elected a member of the Royal Yacht Squadron that year so for the first time *Gossip* sailed under the White Ensign.

They had a calm uneventful crossing to Guernsey and after two days at St. Peter Port continued south past the Roches Douvres to the coast of France. They planned to make Tréguier in the evening but as they entered the river which leads up to the town, Dambom went below to tinker with the engine, leaving the helmsman on deck to navigate between the river booms. Five minutes passed. Suddenly there was an on-ominous bump and a shudder ran through the ship. Dambom abandoned the engine and shot up on deck. He saw at once that *Gossip* was aground on the wrong side of one of the river marks and as the tide was falling he realized she would probably remain there for some hours. Almost at once, and without a word to the man at the wheel, he disappeared below leaving the perplexed helmsman wondering if he was in such disgrace that he was being ignored. Before he had time to get really worried however, Dambom reappeared clutching a bundle of blue bunting.

'Here, just change over the ensigns will you,' he said, chucking the Blue Ensign at the helmsman. 'I'll switch burgees.'

When the operation was completed Dambom laid out the kedge in the deep water so that as soon as *Gossip* refloated he would be able to heave her into the main channel. They spent several uncomfortable hours lying in the river mud before the tide turned and they could pull themselves off with the kedge and continue their passage to Tréguier. Next morning the White Ensign was once more flying over the stern.

From Tréguier they sailed westward with a fair wind hoping to make Roscoff in the six hours before the tide turned against them. Suddenly, after an hour's sailing, as so often happens on the north coast of Brittany, the fog came down and enveloped them, blotting out the coastline. Dambom was just able to take a bearing astern on the great lighthouse of Les Heaux, when that too disappeared in the fog. *Gossip* sailed steadily on her course into unseen waters for two or three hours when Philip, as lookout in the bow, spotted rocks ahead. Dambom identified these as the outriders of Les Sept Iles. He was gifted with a wonderful photographic memory. Once he had seen a silhouette of rocks marking a passage or the leading marks for entering a harbour, he could recall them to sight even after a lapse of years, which is probably why people who didn't know him well thought he had a casual approach to navigation.

After leaving Les Sept Iles Dambom set another course and with Bess steering they continued until he thought he identified the land close to the entrance to Morlaix where a small fishing boat was casting her nets. They sailed close to the land hoping to pick out the beacon which marks the Duslen channel. After continuing on this course for twenty minutes and sighting nothing they gybed round and returned on a reciprocal course until they picked up the small fishing boat once more. This time Dambom called out to the owner asking where they were. The man waved his arms in great excitement and called out 'C'est très dangereuse ici, c'est très dangereuse.'

'Où est Roscoff?' called Dambom.

'Mon dieu, où est Roscoff,' repeated the Frenchman and coming up alongside *Gossip* he leapt on board leaving his mate alone in the boat, seized the wheel from Bess and proceeded to steer between some alarming-looking rocks which nobody seemed to have noticed before.

It turned out that *Gossip* was right amongst the rocks outside the Ile de Batz in a most treacherous area which even the fisherman considered 'dangereuse'. He guided them safely into Roscoff harbour, rapidly followed by his mate and after both boats were moored alongside the quay the whisky bottle was produced. A drink was all the men would accept which is typical of the friendly Bretons.

The fog cleared the next day and *Gossip* continued on her way round the rocky coast of Finistere calling at L'Aberwrac'h and Camaret and then round the Pointe du Raz and on to Loctudy. It was here that *Gossip* changed her crew. Dambom saw Bess and Philip off on the country bus in the morning and was ready to welcome my cousin Ronald and me the same evening.

This crew changing was a chancy business but it never went wrong. A day was selected for the change over before the cruise started but no clue was given as to where the change should take place. The day before the new crew were due to leave England, they received a telegram from Dambom bearing one word only, the name of the place where *Gossip* was lying. It was then left to the relief crew to find the place on the map and work out the best way to reach it in the day.

On this occasion Ronald and I met on the *Falaise*, the night boat from Southampton to St. Malo, and I told him the password was 'Loctudy'. We each had a kitbag of gear to carry and as no bunks were available on the ship we slept on the deck using our kitbags for pillows. Not the best of nights before embarking on a bus trip across Brittany but we survived. We found some other yachtsmen at St. Malo who were bound for Benodet and worked out our route together. We all went to Quimper by bus and then after two hours' delay Ronald and I caught the local bus to Loctudy and left our friends to take the grander and much quicker bus to Benodet. We stopped at each little village and there was a long pause at each stop with much coming and going. The women, laden with baskets of vegetables, dragged their children up the steps. The men, chatting and arguing in good Breton dialect followed empty-handed. Eventually at five o'clock we rattled into the square at Loctudy and found Dambom there to welcome us.

Gossip looked very inviting lying at anchor in the harbour, cool and tranquil. After our long hot journey we lost no time in humping our packs into the dinghy and rowing out to her.

We had a splendid night's sleep and were under way by ten o'clock. With topsail set and the balloon foresail drawing we made for the Ile de Groix. This is a most attractive island, less sophisticated than the popular Belle Ile. Starfish crawl over the harbour

walls and even wend their tortuous way up the
landing steps. At low water they lurk like giant
spiders awaiting their prey on the incoming tide. We
had difficulty in landing and had to pick our way
carefully to avoid treading on an outstretched
tentacle. Once ashore, we climbed the cliff
overlooking the harbour and found a botanist's
paradise. There were hedges of yellow broom and
honeysuckle banked by valerian and campion and
close to the rocks carpets of thrift with pink stone-
crop, sheeps bit scabious and clumps of silver
ragwort. As we penetrated further inland the
vegetation became more lush and the wild flowers
bloomed in profusion.

From the Ile de Groix, we sailed towards Belle Ile.
The sun continued to shine and we drank muscadet at
noon before lunching off langoustine, crisp bagettes
and fresh peaches.

During the afternoon we sailed through the sardine-
fishing fleet and took in our balloon foresail to check
our speed so that we could examine them more
closely. Each fishing boat had a two-manned dinghy
in attendance and it seemed to us that the dinghy
crew threw out a ground bait before returning to their
mother ship. The 'filet-bleu' was then lowered from
the fishing boat and floated in a great semi-circle
supported by little cork floats d round one side of the
ship. Gradually, when the time came, the net was
hauled in by the entire crew, about ten men, and soon
we could see the small silver fish shining in the blue
nets. They continued to pull slowly and carefully
until there was a mass of silver fish leaping and
jumping in the net. At this stage, one of the men took
a long-handled scoop and ladled them out of the net
into the hull of the ship. When some of the weight of
fish had been removed the whole net was taken in.

Entering Le Palais harbour in Belle Ile is always
rather an anxiety as a special style of mooring has to
be carried out. All yachts anchor facing the town
quay and then moor their sterns to the mole or outer

sea wall. As we sailed in flying the White Ensign
with our topsail set and no engine, I heard a voice
saying, 'Now, let's see how the Royal Yacht
Squadron do it!'

It was hectic getting in the sails as we rounded up to
anchor, but I just spied Roger Pinckney on his lovely
yacht *Dyarchy* before I leapt into the dinghy with my
coil of rope to make the stern line fast to the chain on
the mole.

We went on board *Dyarchy* later in the evening and
Roger, a flag-officer of the Royal Cruising Club, told
us that he had filmed our entrance in *Gossip* and
hoped to show it to us at a later date.

After dinner we made an excursion on to the mole
to jettison Thomas into the sea. As we stood on the
wall the orange and green sunset over the Vauban
Citadelle was magnificent and to complete the
picture a full moon in all its splendour rose from the
rocks and the great golden globe was framed
between the port and starboard lighthouses guarding
the harbour entrance. A night to be remembered and
looked back upon through the years.

From Belle Ile we sailed to the Bay of Quiberon
and into the Mer Morbihan. The entrance, close to
Port Navalo, is hazardous due to the supernatural
tides. These run at eight knots during springs and we
had hit them at their strongest. Sailing in the
Morbihan is never dull. The navigation is intricate at
all times and with the fantastic tide it develops into a
battle of wits; man against the moon. There is
nothing straightforward about the sailing. One
minute we were swirling past an island and expecting
to hold the fair tide in the next bend, when we found
ourselves held in the vice-like grip of the maelstrom
between two islands where the tide had taken an
unorthodox course. A man was calmly fishing in a
yellow boat close to the rocks but when he saw our
plight he beckoned to us to come inside him,
between his boat and the rocks. We altered course
and swirled under his stern with frightening rapidity

and then crept through the gap inch by inch. Again we were held by the tide and this time the yellowboated man pointed out to the middle of the channel and surprisingly enough there was a back eddy there where the seaweed had collected and we sailed through.

We anchored for the night off Les Rechauds on the Ile aux Moines. The following morning was Sunday and we went for a walk ashore. As we climbed the hill of the main street we were delighted to find the road decorated with flower patterns, green leaves and sprays of wild honeysuckle. I made enquiries from one of the onlookers and was told it was a 'Pardon' or religious procession for the children. We walked on towards the church and the flower arrangements became more elaborate. One design consisted of a large circle made of daisy heads, the centre being filled with rose petals. As we reached the church the clock chimed eleven and the priest came out into the forecourt and entered a throne made of a canopy surmounted on four poles topped with plumes and carried by four men. As soon as he stood within the throne the bar behind him was shut, as though he was a racehorse entering a box. He was followed out of the church by a host of tiny children, the little girls in their best dresses which were short enough to show off their frilly lace pants, and the little boys spotless in white shorts and brightly coloured shirts. They were lovely children, some of the tiny girls had elaborate hair styles and painted toe-nails peeping out of their coloured sandals and all carried little baskets of rose petals like a host of bridal attendants. Two radiant nuns controlled the procession and when the mothers in national costume and the fathers and elder brethren had walked by I asked one of them if we could join in. She nodded and smiled her agreement. We all processed through the village pausing at two altars set up in the street, where the priest emerged from his throne and offered up prayers while the censer swayed and the little

children scattered rose petals at his feet. I was well
up in the procession and singing lustily in the chorus
which I had just mastered, when Ronald, being of a
more practical nature, hauled me out from my place
beside the elder brethren and led me into a nearby
charcuterie, saying that we had nothing for lunch and
what about it, didn't I think the 'terrine' looked very
appetizing? Reluctantly, I produced the ship's money
and brought myself back to reality and hungry men.

We spent our last day in the Morbihan sailing
amongst the islands and up the famous oyster river
towards Aurey. It is said that all the flat oysters in
France are actually born in the Morbihan. As we
sailed up the river we saw the white lime-washed
tiles which are specially placed to attract the tiny
oysters. The babies measure only three-tenths of a
millimetre when hatched and will then attach
themselves to the tiles as they drift by. Some months
later they are taken from these tiles and placed in the
beds. When they reach the correct size they are sent
to 'nurseries' to mature and go through the purifying
centre or 'dégorgeoir' where they learn to hold sea-
water in their shells when they close their valves.

Perhaps we were looking too hard at the oyster
beds, for when we were about a mile from the town
of Aurey we went aground, and there we stayed,
lying on our beam ends for six hours. Dinner ashore
was out of the question so I had the unpleasant task
of cooking dinner with the boat lying over at an
angle Of 45 degrees. Ronald started shelling the peas
on deck but although I have never known him to be
sea-sick he said he felt too ill to continue the job.

We left the Morbihan the following day and
reluctantly turned for home. We spent another night
in Loctudy but this time we knew no peace. A gale
got up during the night and we seemed to swirl round
and round on our anchor. The harbour was full of
fishing boats and one of these crashed into us in the
early hours of the morning. We all came on deck in
our various night attires, cursing in our various

languages and only returning to our bunks as the
fisherman pulled himself clear. Three hours later we
were roused again, this time our noisy neighbour was
going out fishing. As he swung up alongside
crushing our poor dinghy, a blow from which it
never really recovered, he called out 'Whisky please
monsieur'.

The wind was nearly gale force that morning, so
after breakfast we decided to move across the
harbour to the quieter anchorage off Ile Tudy to get
away from the fishing fleet. Dambom and Ronald
started heaving in the anchor but it was soon evident
that it was foul of something. I added my weight but
it didn't give an inch. There was a large dredger in
the harbour and we thought we had probably hooked
on to her chain, so I went ashore to consult the
captain and after a lot of talking, most of which I
couldn't understand, I gathered that he would come
on board after his siesta, at two o'clock.

We hung about all the morning and sure enough,
promptly at two o'clock the captain brought a small
tug alongside, and taking our anchor chain, he
transferred it to his power-driven winch and set it in
motion. Slowly, slowly the chain came up, fathoms
and fathoms of cable, until gradually we pulled from
the bottom of the harbour the most enormous anchor
I had ever seen and wound round and round one of
its flukes was *Gossip*'s chain and tiny C.Q.R. anchor
looking no bigger than a toy in comparison.
Dambom had to sit out on the bobstay and unravel
the 'knitting'. No wonder we had been twirling round
all night!

Gossip lay in the snug anchorage off Ile Tudy for
three nights while the gale raged outside and on the
fourth morning, well reefed, we sailed out for
Penmarc'h, the first of the great points of Finisterre.
The sea was very lumpy and the waves a great
height, but the wind had died down and we were able
to shake out the reefs. As we passed the Men Hir

rock, we threw the contents of Thomas overboard as
we always liked to sacrifice to the Men Hirs.

We made good progress with a fair southerly wind
and reached the dreaded Pointe du Raz at slack water
as planned. The race off this point is terrifying during
spring tides and it is essential to reach it at slack
water. Even so, after the gales, the seas were
frightening, rolling up astern of us and crashing
along level with the deck, then sweeping over the
bow, white and foaming. They seemed to come from
all directions, boiling and surging around us as
though we were an insect in a witch's cauldron.

We had intended to make for Camaret but with
wind and tide in our favour and being three days
behind schedule, we decided to go right on through
the Chenal du Four.

Saint-Mathieu, the third of the great points, was in a
truculent mood, but we were carried through the
rough seas by the strong tide and *Gossip* sailed on to
the fourth and last point where the Portsall lighthouse
stands out on the reef of rocks. Unfortunately, we
lost the tide and we rolled in the great seas with the
lighthouse abeam, making very little headway.
Dambom said the waves were the biggest he had ever
sailed through and certainly it was astonishing to see
a fishing boat quite close to us at one moment and
then disappearing, mast and all, in the trough of a
great wave. After this statement he retired below to
read his detective book as he said we might wallow
off the point for hours.

Luckily this was not to be our fate. I edged *Gossip*
through the foul tide with her mainsail right out and
drawing well although the boom swung and snarled
in the swell and I dreaded a gybe. I blessed the tall
Vierge lighthouse when it appeared as I knew we
were round the point and Ronald called Dambom
from his book to navigate us into L'Aberwrac'h.
Darkness was falling, but under the kindly light of La
Vierge and with the leading lights in line up the
L'Aberwrac'h River we came safely through the

rocky entrance and anchored off the lifeboat station in the river. After twelve hours' sailing, rolling and vomiting in an active sea, the anchorage seemed like a river of heaven and I have always had a great affection for L'Aberwrac'h which gave us shelter that night.

Some harbours are easier to make after dark and I think L'Aberwrac'h is one of these. As we sailed out next morning through the tangle of rocks it seemed incredible that we had found our way through them in the dark, guided only by the leading lights and the watchful eye of La Vierge standing on her rocky island.

Ronald reminded me of an episode on an earlier trip when *Gossip* was approaching L'Aberwrac'h through the narrow Maloine passage. Suddenly Dambom sighted a yacht which appeared to be heading straight for the rocks.

'Fetch the foghorn and signal "you are running into danger!"' he yelled to Bess, who was the third member of the crew.

She was on deck again in a minute brandishing the foghorn and thumbing through *Reed's Nautical Almanac* for the correct signal.

'"U"' she muttered, and in terrible ignorance of the morse code (in spite of having gained her boatswain's badge as a Girl Guide) proceeded to signal 'V' on the foghorn, three short blasts and one long, which being interpreted means 'I require immediate assistance'.

The yacht gybed smartly in the narrow channel and came towards *Gossip* ready to help a fellow countryman in distress.

Ronald, who was still serving in the Eastern Telegraphic, and fancied his morse shouted to Bess 'You signalled "V"!'

'Yes,' said Dambom, not hearing properly, 'send "B".'

Bess wasted no time in signalling 'B', one long and three short blasts, which means 'I am discharging explosives'. Simultaneously *Gossip*'s engine, always unpredictable, released a violent discharge of black smoke and blue vapour from the exhaust and after uttering two explosive backfires, ground to a halt as a piece of rust flaked off blocking the exhaust pipe.

'For God's sake, what are you signalling now?' shouted Dambom. 'She coming right up to us.'

Bess lost her nerve and bolted below, still clutching *Reed*'s and the foghorn. Dambom followed hastily and it was left to Ronald, alone on deck, to explain to the yacht - if any explanation was possible - that we didn't need assistance but were worried about her.

They met the owner ashore in the evening and found he was so familiar with the coast that he was entering the far more intricate passage to L'Aber-Benoît when *Gossip*'s alarming signals attracted him. The yacht was the *Release;* built to the design of four men who planned her when they were in a prison-of-war camp in Japan during the war.

From L'Aberwrac'h we sailed to Roscoff, the home of the onion men, and anchored off the Ile de Batz, and the following day made Tréguier. Unfortunately, we were behind schedule and Ronald had to leave us there and return to London.

Dambom and I set off alone next morning down the lovely Tréguier River. The engine was giving a lot of trouble and before we were clear of the entrance it seized up for good. Luckily we had a fair wind, light at first, but gradually increasing as the day wore on. We sailed slowly past the terrible Roches Douvres, and set our course for Guernsey.

When we were about ten miles from St. Martin's Point on the south of the island, the wind increased to about Force 6 and Dambom put three rolls in the mainsail and took in the jib and foresail, replacing them with the little storm jib. Under this reduced canvas she sailed well but we hit a squall as we rounded St. Martin's Point and the storm jib tore in two places and flapped maddeningly. Dambom put two more rolls in the mainsail to make her more

manoeuvrable and as we approached the entrance to
St. Peter Port, where the harbour master stands in
command and shouts at every yacht as she comes in,
telling her where to anchor, he disappeared below
saying, 'You sail her in and I'll stay out of sight until
you are clear of the entrance. The harbour master
won't shout at a lone woman and then we can go
where we like.'

Gossip must have looked a sorry sight with her
storm jib flapping, her main well-reefed and a damp
and tousle-haired woman wrestling with the wheel.
The strategy worked perfectly. No one shouted, and
once safely in the harbour, Dambom shot up out of
the fore-hatch and directed me to his chosen
anchorage.

As soon as the hook was down and we had
collected and stowed our sails, we received a hail
from a British submarine moored alongside the quay
and Alan Turvill, a young sub-lieutenant from
Yarmouth, who had watched our entry with great
interest, invited us to come on board. Still rolling
from our rough passage we rowed out to visit him
and after clambering up the rounded side of the
submarine we had a well-earned drink in the tiny
wardroom.

We had had a strenuous day and while we were
having dinner ashore later that evening Dambom said
we would have a holiday next day and rest before our
passage across the channel.

The morning of our holiday dawned warm and
sunny and I planned a peaceful day reading on deck
and tidying up the ship. I was surprised to see that
most of the yachts in the harbour were dressed
overall but this was soon explained to me by a man
in a passing dinghy who handed me a programme
saying it was the annual Regatta and he would be
delighted if we would join in the festivities. Dambom
was dismantling the torn jib at that moment, but he
came across and said we would be very pleased to

take part in their Regatta. He then took the programme from me and studied the items.

'That's the one for us,' he said. 'Rowing race, one lady, one gent. You start mending the jib straight away while I look out the flags and dress the ship.'

By the time we had sorted the flags and hoisted them in the approved manner it was eleven o'clock. I sat down on the deck with the jib spread out around me and mended the two tears with the only thing I could find, strips torn from my brother's farm trousers which I found by chance in the paint locker. This took me the rest of the morning and then Dambom hailed me from the dinghy where he was struggling with the large tin jerrycan which he had just filled with water from the quay.

'We must have some ballast in the stern,' he said. 'Hop in and we'll have a trial row round the harbour.'

All went well on the trials, although the dinghy was leaking badly, thanks to the fishermen at Loctudy, but we barely had time for lunch as our event was due to start at two o'clock.

When our great moment arrived we rowed up to the start in the inner harbour in splendid style and at the crack of the pistol we were away. Unfortunately, there was rather a large entry in our class and one dinghy charged us in the general mêlée forcing us to spin round in a circle. Dambom, of course, was undaunted and we made a second start and were soon striking away from the tangle of small boats still rotating round the starting line. We rowed well together, after years of experience, and certainly the jerrycan balanced the boat, but we had one deadly rival, a much, much younger couple and it was a fierce fight to the finish. We hit the rope at the far end of the inner harbour as we surged across the finishing line, worthy of any event at Henley, just half a length ahead of our young opponents.

After the celebrations and fireworks in the evening
we retired thankfully to our bunks, exhausted after
our day of rest.

The tides around the Channel Islands are only
surpassed by those of the Morbihan, so it was
essential with our lack of engine, that we made the
most of them. Accordingly, next morning we left the
harbour in time to get the fair tide in the Petit Russel.
We drifted out of the harbour under mainsail and jib,
acknowledging the watching sentinel of the harbour
master on this occasion, and then Dambom set the
balloon foresail and the topsail as we needed to
attract every breath of wind. Even so, our passage
was very slow and when we were through the Petit
Russel we decided to put into Alderney for the night
and hope for a better breeze the following day to help
us across the Channel. The tide was fair in the
Swinge as we altered course to the eastward. I was
steering for Bray harbour and at the same time trying
to look at the colony of gannets which had recently
taken over the small rocky island of Ortac. I was
definitely more interested in watching these clean-
diving aristocratic gulls than in steering the drifting
ship and Dambom soon came on deck to join me in
my bird-watching. Suddenly he realized that we were
being drawn towards Ortac by unseen hands. He
hurried below and examined the chart and tide table
leaving me to bear away from the rock and make for
the Alderney shore. It was no use, we were being
sucked nearer and nearer to the rock. Dambom shot
up on deck again and said, 'the book says that in
certain conditions the tide sets out towards Ortac on
the last hour of the flood.'

He surveyed the scene which was now becoming
desperate. We were being drawn stern first steadily
nearer and nearer to the rock. There was nothing we
could do except wait and hope and pray.

'We'll be wrecked,' muttered Dambom as he stood
firmly in the hatchway. 'There's no chance of
missing the rock.'

It was the first time in all the years I had sailed with
him that he had ever taken a pessimistic view and I
was in a panic. I realized that with the strong tide and
the heavy swell our boat would be smashed to pieces
once we hit the rock. I wanted to ask for the
lifejackets and to find out if there was a lifeboat in
Alderney but my throat had dried up so I just sat
there, hearing the birds all around me, willing *Gossip*
to make some headway. The rock was so close I
could have hit it with a biscuit. The sides were
smooth and rounded and covered with guano. There
wasn't a foothold and the angry birds, so beautiful a
few minutes ago, now looked fierce and menacing.
The swell rose and fell and we moved up and down
with it getting closer and closer with every wave.
Suddenly a breath of wind filled the topsail; then the
mainsail. The balloon foresail puffed out and we held
our own. Dambom still stood in the hatchway. I still
held the wheel. We didn't speak. We didn't move.
Very gradually we edged away from the rock. Inch
by inch and foot by foot we moved until we were
clear of its magnetic field. We breathed again. We
spoke again and I edged *Gossip* clear of the Swinge.

Dambom was full of confidence at once and
reckoned the tide would finish soon and we could try
to make Alderney once more. I knew I couldn't go
through all that again so soon and suggested we
sailed towards the Casquets and on for home. There
was very little wind and it might mean a night of
drifting, but I said I would be happy to steer and keep
watch for the greater part of the night; so we set a
course for the Casquets and Dambom went below
and cooked dinner.

It was a perfect evening and I have always enjoyed
night sailing in fine weather. I like the loneliness and
the peace and the mysteries lying behind the many
lights and ships that move away in the darkness. I
recite poetry and even sing when there is no one to
hear me. So when Dambom left me alone at midnight

I sipped my cocoa and surveyed the starry universe with pleasurable anticipation.

We had taken down the topsail and changed foresails before dark in case the wind increased in the night. We needn't have worried, the Casquets were still in sight at dawn. We made less than five miles during the hours of darkness. There was quite a lot of shipping in the vicinity and I had one scare during the night when I heard the thrum of engines somewhere behind me. I realized I was scarcely visible to a boat dead astern of me with only my port and starboard lights showing, so I reached quickly for the big torch and flashed it on the white sail. The engines stopped and almost at once the ship appeared. She was much closer than I had realized and I had probably given her a terrible shock. She started her engines again and circled right round *Gossip*, probably cursing us for not having more lights showing and then, just as suddenly as she had come, she disappeared into the darkness.

Luckily the breeze increased with the daylight and with topsail set once more we made a very good crossing and by the time we sighted Needles at nine o'clock in the evening we were heeling over with a strong westerly wind. We held the fair tide through the Solent and anchored off Yarmouth an hour later. We took down the sails and had a belated dinner below, and were just thinking longingly of our bunks when Dambom went on deck to put up the riding light and realized that our anchor was dragging and we were being carried by the ebb towards Black Rock. Hastily we set the foresail and mainsail and took in the anchor cable and sailed up to our anchorage once more. This time all was well and we slept in peace until the Customs launch came alongside early the next morning.

1955 – Man Overboard

Alan was demobilized on his twenty-first birthday, October 6th 1947. He had no clear idea at this time of what he wanted to do but after working his way round Australia and New Zealand, he returned to England and studied farming for several years before deciding to settle on the Island, and run his own small dairy farm.

He was due to take over his farm at Michaelmas 1955, and as he had several weeks free that summer, he, and his friend Charlie Dodd, who had toured Australia with him, volunteered to crew for Dambom on a trip to Brittany.

While Dambom worked fitting out *Gossip*, Alan travelled round the country studying cattle prices at the various markets. He returned from one of these jaunts announcing that he had found a real bargain which he couldn't resist. The 'bargain', in the form of five Jersey heifers and a Jersey cow, duly arrived on the ferry that same afternoon. With only a week before the cruise was due to start, this little herd, with their deer-like eyes and golden coats, were a slight embarrassment to him, but having promised to crew for Dambom he couldn't let him down at the last minute. Luckily, just before *Gossip* sailed, one of his friends offered to look after them, and keep them in her boss's field with his herd of Guernseys.

It was early in June when *Gossip*, with Dambom and the two boys, finally left Yarmouth, and after clearing the Needles, Charlie, who was a complete newcomer to sailing, was given some instruction on steering and the general running of the ship. He asked a number of questions, and Dambom was impressed by his keenness to learn, and his general intelligence. Together they hoisted the topsail and the balloon foresail, while Alan steered on a course for Alderney - a distance of sixty miles.

After keeping this course for several hours, and gaining about twenty miles, the wind freshened from the south-west, and the swell, always present in the Channel, became so vicious that Alan succumbed to seasickness and retired below. Charlie, now quite at home at the wheel, was unperturbed and took over the steering while Dambom handed the topsail. Suddenly he was jerked out of his equilibrium by the sound of a splash, and the next second he saw Dambom in the sea, clad in his heavy yellow oilskins, already drifting astern of the moving yacht.

Shouting 'Man overboard!' he picked up the lifebuoy and threw it over the stern within a few feet of the stunned man, as the yacht swept ahead, leaving the small yellow figure bobbing up and down in the swell.

This single act above all others, saved Dambom's life, and as *Gossip* sailed away from him he struggled to reach the cord loop on the buoy. Even two or three strokes in his dazed condition, pulled down by his heavy oilskins, seemed a tremendous

effort, but his fingers touched the cord at last and he
pulled the heavy ring over his head and, pushing his
neck back against the hard canvas he rested, with his
arms across the lifebuoy, thus keeping his head
above the waves.

Was it chance, or fate, that had prompted Charlie to
ask Dambom, only two hours before, what he should
do if such an emergency arose? No one to his
knowledge had ever asked such an essential question
before, and no one had ever fallen overboard when
Gossip was sailing, in all the years he had owned her.

Alan was on deck in an instant. His first act was to
try and gybe the ship, but the balloon foresail, caught
by a sudden gust of wind, tore like tissue paper and
fluttered and beat itself against the rigging, like a
bird imprisoned in a cage. Without letting out the
main sheet she wouldn't gybe and this he didn't like
to risk in the stiff breeze. Quickly he changed tactics
and brought *Gossip* into the wind, trying to check her
speed before she travelled any further from the
desperate man in the water.

The flapping of the shredded foresail made her
difficult to handle, so Charlie ripped it down,
thrusting it under the anchor chain, and eventually
she came round and checked her way.

Alan now decided to launch the dinghy before they
drifted any further from the crucial spot. Cutting the
lashings which held it on deck, he freed it from its
bonds, while Charlie threw out all the extraneous
gear which had been stored there for the passage,
including coils of rope, fenders, petrol cans and the
heavy boom crutch. They had some difficulty in
launching the little boat in the lumpy sea. If they
pushed her over the gunwale, stern first, in the usual
way, she would have filled instantly, so they lifted
her bodily, and threw her over the side of the ship, so
that she landed like a cork on the summit of the
waves. They were strong young men, even so,
desperation must have given them extra strength.

They would have found this a Herculean task without
the impetus of fear.

By now there was no sign of Dambom. There was
no sign of land. There was no sign of a ship on the
horizon, and there was no sound above the breaking
of the waves. They were desperately alone, thinking
only of Dambom, somewhere, in that vast emptiness.

By the aid of the compass and the feel of the wind,
they worked out the most likely area in which to
search. The decision as to who should go in the
dinghy was quickly resolved. Charlie, although he
had scarcely rowed before, volunteered for the job.
He said Alan knew how to start the engine, and being
the more experienced crew, should remain in
command of *Gossip*. This was a good decision, as
Charlie was gifted with exceptionally good sight.
Unfortunately, as Alan pushed his friend clear of the
rolling yacht to avoid swamping the dinghy, the iron
block from the lee runner swung out and hit him
across the forehead and, as he pulled away, the blood
streamed down his face.

Struggling with the oars for the first few minutes,
and wiping the blood from his eyes, Charlie forced
himself to control the boat and make headway. After
some steady rowing away from the yacht, his keen
eyes spotted a tiny yellow speck which appeared at
intervals on the crest of the waves. Confident now,
he continued to row, very, very carefully,
concentrating on each stroke, fearful that he might
lose an oar, or swamp the little boat. When he finally
reached Dambom, he found him numbed with cold,
inert and speechless, and too weak to help himself.
Pulling the oars back in the dinghy, Charlie reached
out and clutched the lifebuoy. As he leant over the
side a wave sloshed up, nearly sinking his boat. He
realized he would never get Dambom aboard this
way. Still grasping the lifebuoy, he guided it round to
the stern and made it fast to the after-painter. Now he
had command of the situation, and gripping Dambom
firmly under his arms, he dragged him bodily over

the transom. Buttons popped off the unconscious man's oilskin as he was heaved on board but Charlie had him safely in the boat at last, and laid him down on the floor boards.

Alan, meanwhile, was struggling with the engine down below, desperate to start the reluctant brute. Unaware of how things were going with Charlie, he cranked and cranked while the sweat from his forehead dripped into the bilge, and the gorge rose in his throat. Eventually, after many false stutters, the engine broke into life. Pushing the gear lever forward he hurried on deck, and grasping the wheel, steered for the small bouncing dinghy, now nearly a quarter of a mile away. Once on course, he left the boat to steer herself and lowered the mainsail, which all this time had been lashing about, and would make coming alongside single-handed a difficult manoeuvre. Dashing some tyers round the unmanageable sail, he returned to the wheel and came up as close as he dared to the dinghy, which was rolling about in the heavy swell. He then put the engine in neutral, and called to Charlie to row the boat alongside. At his first attempt he came too near the stern and the dinghy caught under *Gossip*'s counter and was nearly swamped once more by an oncoming wave. Alan grabbed the painter and pulled the little boat up amidships before making it fast on the jib-sheet cleat. Charlie made fast the stern line. Then began the task of lifting the unconscious man out of the dinghy and getting him on board *Gossip*, whilst the boat rose and fell with the waves and dashed itself against the side of the ship. Finally, on the upsurge of a wave, Charlie lifted Dambom bodily from the dinghy, and Alan half dragged, half lifted him over the rail to the comparative security of the deck.

By this time the boys were alarmed and exhausted. Dambom lay on the deck, shrunken, grey and apparently lifeless. They lowered him down the steep companionway, and after undressing him, they rolled him in blankets and laid him on the settee. He was so cold and inert that they despaired of ever bringing him round, but after about twenty minutes, he managed to ask for a barley sugar which seemed to get his saliva working again, and from that moment he never looked back.

Dambom never knew how he fell overboard. He said he suddenly found himself in the sea, and only just managed to reach the lifebuoy as Charlie threw it over. He knew panic when he *saw Gossip* sailing away from him, realizing the inexperience of the boys. He watched the balloon foresail flying aloft, and he watched Charlie getting into the dinghy. He knew they couldn't see him low down in the water. He tried to shout, but his feeble voice sounded to him like the faint, whining squawk of a gull. He knew Charlie had hardly rowed before and he doubted if he would ever reach him in the lumpy sea. At this stage of thinking, his senses became numbed by the cold and he couldn't even call out to his rescuer.

Some time after they had picked him up and he had sucked his barley sugar and had a glass of sherry, he looked at the tell-tale compass, and saw *Gossip* was heading north-east.

'What on earth are you doing?' he called to Alan 'You're right off course.'

'I'm heading back to Yarmouth.'

'Oh no thank you, we're not going back there. We'll go to Poole if you like, but not Yarmouth, and don't you dare tell your mother!'

They spent that night in Poole harbour. Dambom had recovered by the evening, but decided to stay on board while the boys went ashore for dinner. As an after-thought, just as they were leaving, he handed them his salt-sodden clothes.

'You might rinse these through in the cloakroom,' he said.

The next morning they set out again, and this time they made Alderney. Dambom was in his seventy-sixth year at the time, but within twenty-four hours of the near tragedy he was roaring with laughter about the whole episode, and especially the boy's account of their arrival at the smart hotel clutching a large bundle of wet clothes, which they proceeded to wash in the small basin in the 'gent's' cloakroom.

From the Channel Islands they sailed to Tréguier and then along the Brittany coast down as far as the Mer Morbihan. Disaster seemed to follow disaster, but all were of a minor variety compared with the incident in the Channel. Sailing up the river to Morlaix, against the wind, they went too close to the bank, and had to spend a very uncomfortable eight hours with *Gossip* lying on her beam ends.

At L'Aberwrac'h they encountered fog and lay at anchor for twenty-four hours, with one of the old Victorian bells taken from the servant's hall at Norlands hanging in the rigging. This was their only guide to finding *Gossip* again after a dinner ashore. Luckily the faint swell in the river was just sufficient to raise a tinkle in the bell, which instead of summoning a maid to a guestroom, as had been its role at Norlands, now guided the men back to the yacht.

Also at L'Aberwrac'h they lost their anchor. Heaving it in.' the morning after the fog, with all hands working, they failed to move it. Dambom decided the only thing to do was to abandon it but naturally didn't want to lose more cable than was absolutely necessary. So, with the chain held hard and fast on deck, he produced a small Woolworth's hack-saw, about six inches long, from the tool locker, and proceeded to saw through one of the half inch links. Each man in turn took a spell at this gruelling job, and eventually, like releasing a manacled prisoner, the anchor was freed. Before letting the chain go, Dambom was careful to attach a marker-buoy on a length of rope, in the hope of retrieving the anchor at a later date. Unfortunately when he returned to L'Aberwrac'h on the homeward journey, the marker-buoy had disappeared.

Gossip carried a spare fisherman's anchor which was used for the rest of the voyage. Later this was replaced by the modern, and comparatively lighter, C.Q.R. anchor.

Their last mishap before the return journey was when they anchored on top of a huge concrete sinker in Port Maria harbour, at the entrance of the Mer Morbihan. They were made hideously aware of this at four in the morning when they were awoken by a heavy bumping under the keel, which repeated itself with the steady rhythm of a funeral drum. Immediately all hands were on deck, and Dambom and Charlie took the kedge in the dinghy and laid it out in the deep water, while Alan paid out the warp after leading it through the fairlead. The combined strength of the three men was sufficient to pull the yacht clear before any serious damage was done to her keel.

This was the last of their troubles. The boys returned to England a few days later, leaving Dambom with his relief crew, Ronald Saxby and Philip Cheverton, to bring *Gossip* back to Yarmouth.

Alan, who is superstitious by nature, felt there was some truth in the adage that it is unlucky to take a parson in a ship. He claimed that Charlie, who was a theological student at Cambridge at the time, might be responsible for their ill luck. This I considered an unfair assumption. Charlie was as much farmer as priest at the time, also it was due to his good sense, strength and exceptional eyesight that Dambom was rescued from his ordeal in the Channel.

While Dambom and his crew were engaged in high drama in the Channel, the 'girls' were having their own drama at Norlands. Bess received a telephone call a few days after *Gossip*'s departure, from the girl Alan had entrusted with his cows, saying that her boss had returned and had been horrified at finding six sickly cows mingling with his splendid herd of Guernseys and would we please remove them forthwith.

Bess hastily summoned Lucia and me from our nearby houses, and we set out on the two-mile walk to the farm. When we arrived we realized that the poor animals were indeed sick. They were coughing spasmodically in a dry throaty way, and their golden coats looked stark and unkempt.

As soon as we started driving them along the main Newport-Yarmouth road they seemed to recover their spirits, and the three of us had a lively time trying to control them. Most cows one meets on the road amble along so slowly that they hold up the passing traffic, and mooch along, nosing and snuffling into the car windows. Not so Alan's cows. The young heifers were quite out of control, sometimes skipping across the road regardless of the traffic, and sometimes in full cry like a pack of ravening hounds. Bess and Lucia, who had run in their school relay team, tried to keep ahead of the herd, and check their mad onrush; but I was not made of such stuff and contented myself with looking after Cherry, the old lady of the herd, who was obviously poorly and could hardly drag herself along.

My sisters, with their five frolicking heifers, reached Yarmouth long before me, and took the town at a canter.

Leaving them to cross the bridge to Norlands, I took poor Cherry to the Royal Solent Yacht Club, as I realized we were both in need of a rest. I tethered her to a tree with an odd piece of rope I found in the shed, and the boatman brought her some water in a ship's bucket. While she was enjoying her 'elevenses' I went to look over the bridge, but saw no sign of the others. I hoped they were now safely across, and had not suffered the fate of the Gadarene swine and disappeared into the harbour.

When I returned to the Yacht Club I saw the Commodore eyeing Cherry with considerable apprehension, and he remarked that he had never before seen a cow enjoying the facilities of the Club!

As soon as Cherry had recovered sufficiently, we ambled over the bridge together to the field at Norlands. Bess greeted me with the news that the vet had already been and declared the animals to be suffering from 'husk', a type of bovine bronchitis caused by a nematode, whatever that was. He was most emphatic that they should all be housed indoors and kept off the grass for at least a fortnight. How we blessed our young brother, away on the high seas, oblivious of the fate of his precious cattle.

The stables at Norlands had been in disuse since the advent of the motor-car, and the three of us were faced with the task of clearing them before nightfall. We started on the loose-box which held all the strawberry cages, wheelbarrows, croquet sets, potatoes and bulbs, and all the rotten warps, fenders and old sails which had been discarded from *Gossip*, but not thrown away in case they 'came in useful'. From the loose-box we moved to the stalls, and here we nearly met our match, for stored against the whole of one wall, were volumes and volumes of bound copies of the *Illustrated News*, dating back to the time when the house was built, nearly a hundred years before. The coach house was an easier job, as most of the boats it was wont to harbour were already out.

When all the clearing had been done and some fresh straw and hay obtained from a nearby farm, we started housing the cattle. This was no easy job, as the temperamental heifers 'cut up nasty' and started lashing out with their feet. My friend Cherry, as the old lady of the herd and the one really sick animal, had a 'single room' in the old garage where Bess usually kept her car.

The vet had left a large bottle of physic and with all three of us working together, we were able to 'drench' the cows before leaving them for the night.

For nearly a fortnight we tended the herd, 'drenching' them daily and supplying them with food, water and bedding, and by the time Alan returned, the young heifers were well on their way to recovery, but Cherry never quite got over her attack, and the calf she gave birth to a few weeks later one Sunday afternoon, when the family were gathered on the lawn for the weekly tea-party, was stillborn.

Bathing played a very important part in our way of life on board. Sometimes one bathed out of sheer necessity, as it was the only means of a wholesale ablution during a cruise, which might last as long as six weeks. At other times, and these were much rarer with me as I grew older, one bathed for sheer enjoyment and certainly, on a really hot, windless day, it was pleasant to plunge over the side when *Gossip* was in an idling mood, and catch hold of a rope trailing over the stern and get wafted along in the wake of the ship.

Dambom never missed his morning dip, which he considered a wholesome and hygienic way in which to start the day. I sometimes wondered if he was right, especially in some of the French rivers. I recall one morning when we were cruising in Brittany and *Gossip* was lying at anchor in the Auray River close to the town. Lucia and I had gone ashore early to buy croissants and milk for breakfast and were fascinated to see many of the black-clothed women of the town walking towards the river carrying little white-lidded enamel buckets. We joined the procession when we had done our shopping, intrigued to learn the contents of these new style Thomas's. We weren't left long in doubt; as they reached the bridge, a mere hundred yards from *Gossip*'s mooring, the lids were raised, and the good women of Auray deposited their 'night-soil' in the out-flowing river. We hurried back to the yacht and as we came on board Dambom emerged from the water, reached for the bobstay and climbed up on the bowsprit.

'Very nice,' he said, as he shook himself over the deck. 'Very nice and refreshing. Why don't you girls have a swim?'

Dambom employed another method of bathing
when we were actually sailing. He would lower
himself from the bowsprit on to the bobstay and dip
in the waves as *Gossip* moved through the water. in
gentle seas it was a harmless enough pastime, but
Ronald and I were very alarmed when he decided to
'dip' in this manner one hot afternoon when we were
going through the race off Point de Saint-Mathieu in
the Chenal du Four. There was much more sea than
he expected, and he was immersed at every wave. He
began to show signs of exhaustion as every time he
reached up to regain the bowsprit he was hit by
another wave and pushed under. He clung on like a
limpet, but was soon gasping for breath and
eventually Ronald had to lean out on the bowsprit
and heave him to safety. He never repeated this
hazardous sport unless we were in very calm waters.

Sometimes it was so cold when we were cruising
that Bess and I were apt to forget our bathing dresses
intentionally. She was caught out, however, one
week in Brittany, when the days were so hot that she
longed for a swim. Finally, one scorching afternoon
in Loctudy she could bear it no longer and devised a
costume consisting of a pair of pants, which took
care of the lower half, and a carefully draped scarf
which completed her bikini. She dived over the side
and had a refreshing swim round the ship.
Unfortunately, as she swam, the scarf unwound in
the water, and trailed behind her, like seaweed
caught in a mermaid's tresses. Embarrassed, she
reached for the bobstay, and as she emerged like
Venus from the waves, her scarf fell away, and the
self-same moment two rowing boats, manned by
cadets from L'Ecole Nautique, appeared as if from
nowhere, and the crews rested open-mouthed on their
oars, only ten yards from the yacht, as she climbed
up on to the bowsprit and regained the safety of the
deck, and the seclusion of the cabin.

1956 – Fog in the Channel

In May 1956 the 5.5metre yachts of many nations were assembled at Le Havre to compete in the series of races for the Coppa d'Italia and the Coupe de Paris. The British yacht *Vision*, owned and sailed by Colonel 'Stug' Perry with Desmond and Neil Cochran-Patrick as crew, was a firm favourite for the Cup and Lucia persuaded Dambom that it would be amusing to sail over to Le Havre in *Gossip* to watch the racing.

Bess signed on as the third member of the crew and early in May they crossed the Channel, making for Barfleur on the eastern tip of the Cherbourg peninsula. They made a good landfall, identifying the powerful light off the Point de Barfleur just after midnight. Dambom started the engine as they approached the harbour entrance but almost at once it seized up and *Gossip* was jerked to a standstill. A torch shining over the stern revealed a snake's honeymoon of ropes and corks which were obviously attached to the propeller, so there was nothing for it but to lower the sails and anchor while they sorted it out. This wasn't too easy in the dark but after some hard pulling Dambom and Bess dragged a lobster pot to the surface. Realizing their predicament, close to the entrance of the harbour, they knew they were in danger from the fishing boats coming and going during the night so reluctantly Lucia drew the carving knife and cut the pot adrift.

This only offered a temporary relief as most of the rope was still wound round the propeller shaft putting the engine out of action, so all that night *Gossip* lay at anchor rolling in the heavy swell under the penetrating eye of the Barfleur light.

Early the next morning, after a restless and uncomfortable night, Bess and Lucia worked from the dinghy trying to unravel the lines while Dambom donned his bathing trunks and, armed with a knife, tried to cut away the rope directly round the propeller shaft. Eventually they succeeded in clearing it, but it was of no avail as the engine refused to start.

From Barfleur they sailed to Port-en-Bessin, a tiny village where there were many war victims standing around the quay leaning on crutches or fishing from the harbour wall, their injured limbs propped up on empty crates, their glazed expressions dulled by suffering.

Dambom and his crew took a bus to Bayeux and spent the afternoon revelling in the magic of the Tapestry. They visited Arromanches and saw the concrete moulds which had formed the basis of the Mulberry harbour and identified many of the weird structures which I had seen floating down the Solent when I was working at H.M.S. *Manatee* and which were still lying around as evidence of the great Invasion.

Dambom was sailing with the help of the Royal Cruising Club charts dated 1912, so it was not surprising that forty-four years and two wars later things weren't 'quite what they used to be' and navigation became something of a gamble.

Gossip entered Deauville harbour the following day under full sail as the engine was still out of action, and as she swept through the narrow, unfamiliar entrance Dambom realized that a bridge had been raised to let him through at the crucial moment. Nothing daunted, he shouted to the man on duty that he wanted a mechanic and then rounded up in the harbour with no clear idea where to go. Bess and Lucia lowered the mainsail and rolled up the jib and then, realizing that they were expected to lie stern on to the quay, Dambom dropped the anchor and paid out the stern warp to Bess who was already in the dinghy making for the quay. When they were safely moored Dambom realized that he was now locked into the harbour as the bridge had swung back into position and the lock-gates had closed behind him. Apparently there had been a change in the mooring arrangements since 1912 and the lockgates had been moved from the inner basin to the outer harbour.

Two days later Robin Aisher and Desmond were standing on the Yacht Club balcony at Le Havre when *Gossip*, still with no engine, and using her 1912 charts, entered the busy shipping port through a short cut between the small green wreck buoys.

'Look at that yacht,' said Robin. 'Only a British yacht would come right through the wrecks!'

'Yes,' said Desmond, recognizing *Gossip*. 'And only my father-in-law would do it under full sail.'

As Gossip rounded up in the inner yacht harbour, Dambom realized that he was expected to moor between two buoys. This was no easy task under sail, but before Bess could run out the second warp to the stern buoy a helpful member of the Société des Regattes du Havre (the yacht club overlooking the harbour) came to her aid in a motor-boat and completed the mooring.

They spent a very gay week in Le Havre as guests of the hospitable French yachtsmen under the guidance of Monsieur Cadot. Every day they were taken out in the 'vedette' belonging to the Yacht Club and were able to follow *Vision* round the course, and every night they were royally entertained by the French on shore.

One evening which stood out as a highlight of the week, they visited Fécamp Benedectine Monastery where they were shown round by Monsieur Le Grande, the head of the establishment. After a cocktail, of which the main ingredient was Benedictine and found to be very potent, they had a superb dinner at a 'bistro' in the little village of Yport where they ate six fish courses followed by apple charlotte. The finale of the evening was a return visit to the Monastery at midnight, where they drank the most perfect vintage champagne with Monsieur Le Grande.

The racing was full of excitement for the onlookers in the 'vedette'. *Vision*, sailed superbly by 'Stug' Perry, with Desmond as the calm, unruffled navigator and Neil the fore-deck hand who developed a magic when handling the spinnaker, was the most successful yacht amongst the many nationalities competing for the Cups. She won the first three of the five races, thus assuring herself of the Coppa d'Italia but disaster hit her in the Coupe de Paris when, in the last leg of the final race, her jib split across one of the seams. This gave Monsieur Cadot, in the French yacht *Gilliat V*, a chance to take the lead and win the Cup. *Vision* was a close second after Neil had completed a change of jibs in record time.

Vision was the winner of the series for the Coppa d'Italia but when Monsieur Cadot received the Coupe de Paris at the prize-giving ceremony, he was such a splendid sportsman that he handed Mrs. Perry the replica of the Cup, as he considered *Vision* was the moral winner of the race and he had only won through her mishap.

The successful yacht *Vision* went to Melbourne later that year and 'Stug' Perry, with Desmond and Neil as his crew, brought back the silver medal for Britain.

Sailing in fog is always a frightening experience and *Gossip* had her fair share of it when cruising in the vicinity of Brittany and the Channel Islands where it is prevalent.

One year Dambom with Lucia and Ronald as crew sailed out of L'Aberwrac'h on a sultry morning in June, when suddenly the fog enveloped them shutting out everything. They were in a very dangerous rocky area but even in fog Dambom had a sense of direction and an uncanny way of knowing each rock by name and recognizing it by its shape even after an absence of years. With only the compass to guide them they felt their way round the north-west corner of Brittany although Lucia said that when they saw the Portsall buoy it loomed up so large that she thought it was the lighthouse. The next thing they saw was the great Four lighthouse which suddenly appeared dead ahead when they were almost on the rock and then, just when Dambom had decided that it was impossible to make the Chenal du Four in such conditions, and was preparing to sail out to sea to round Ushant, the fog lifted and they sailed through the intricate channel to Camaret.

Dambom used to tell us that unless we could identify a mark when trying to make a landfall in fog, the only thing to do was to turn back to the open sea on a reciprocal course, and wait until it cleared. Bess and I were to think of this advice when a few years later she was asked to take *Sea Jack* from Yarmouth to Deauville for the owner, Lionel Landon.

Lionel had sailed as a boy with my father, and developed his love of boats and the sea after cruising in *Gossip* in Scandinavian waters.

Sea Jack is a lovely cutter of thirty-five tons with an overall length of fifty-nine feet. She wears a slightly cut down twelve-metre mainsail - which belonged to Norsaga - on her eighty-foot mast.

It was early in May when Bess took command of this splendid yacht. On board as crew were Dr. John Kiszely and his wife Bunty, Philip Cheverton and myself. We were an inadequate crew for such a large ship, and none of us, with the exception of Bess, had ever sailed in her before. John was an excellent helmsman in his small X.O.D. class yacht, but he had scarcely done any cruising, and Bunty, although an experienced crew in the 'X', had never sailed in a larger boat. Philip, who had often crewed for Dambom in *Gossip*, was strong and efficient, and absolutely reliable, but he was the only member of the crew agile enough to run out on the bowsprit every time we set the jib. I signed on as helmsman and Bunty took over duties of cook and stewardess and looked after us admirably throughout the whole trip.

We set sail from Yarmouth at eleven o'clock on the morning of Friday, May 5th, as soon as the doctor had cleared his surgery. The forecast was not promising, with a warning of fog patches in the Channel, but John and Philip were limited for time so we decided to set sail and hope for the best.

Sea Jack must have been a lovely sight as she left Yarmouth. We hoisted the huge white mainsail as soon as we were clear of the harbour, and the jib and foresail followed in quick succession, so that watchers on the quay saw her in all her glory under full sail.

As we passed Norlands, Dambom dipped the flag, and I dipped *Sea Jack*'s ensign in acknowledgement. I wondered what his thoughts were seeing us setting out on our own, but he never worried for long, and he would expect us to do the right thing and make a good landfall.

The Needles was abeam an hour later, and we heard the moaning from the lighthouse tower as the fog rolled in from the Channel and enveloped us.

All day we sailed with a steady north-west wind. It was cold and unpleasant with occasional showers of rain, and the ever persistent fog acting as a depressant. Ships' sirens, sometimes near at hand, and sometimes wailing in the distance, broke the monotony, and sent shivers down my spine. We hoped they had radar. We hadn't. We had nothing. Nothing but the compass to guide us through the folds of cotton wool which isolated us from the outside world.

That evening, nine hours after leaving the Needles, the log registered fifty-seven miles, which left us with only three more to sail before we completed the sixty miles to Cherbourg breakwater. Anxiously, we peered through the fog when suddenly Philip reported a faint flash near our port bow. I luffed up close to the light but it disappeared again, swallowed up in the fog. Bess just managed to count the flashes before it vanished, one flash, a second's pause and another flash, and that was all we ever saw of it.

This was where we made our first mistake. I remember once in *Gossip*, when I sailed fairly close to a buoy but failed to read the name, Dambom made me gybe round and come up closer still so that I could identify it.

It would have taken some time to haul in the sheet and gybe round in *Sea Jack*, but it would certainly have saved us time and worry in the end.

After studying the chart, Bess reckoned it must be La Pierre Noire, a buoy thirteen miles cast of Cherbourg. The wind was increasing, so John and Philip took two rolls in the mainsail and handed the staysail. I steered due west as Bess calculated that with the westerly running tide we should soon see the light on the harbour breakwater if we followed this course. After ten minutes or so the look-out reported seeing a number of faint lights ahead so, thinking this must be the shore, we tacked out to sea and headed north. This seemed the safest course. Dambom would have done this we felt sure. His maxim was always to turn back on a reciprocal course when lost in fog.

The motion got very uncomfortable on the new tack, and even the sturdy thirty-five-tonner rolled and pitched in the lumpy sea.

'I hear a foghorn!' shouted John.

We were all silent, listening. It came again, and we counted the blasts together. Four blasts, a pause for a minute, then four blasts again, and another pause.

'Alderney!' said Bess. 'I know that foghorn only too well from sailing in *Gossip*. There's no doubt about it, and that's why we are in such a rough sea. We are in the Alderney Race.'

She realized too late that she must have been mistaken in her identification of the first buoy. She pored over the chart. It could have been the light buoy off Jardehen Point. That flashed once every 1½ seconds. It lay just to the east of the great lighthouse on the Cap de la Hague. It seemed incredible that we had seen the small flashing buoy and missed the great lighthouse, but fog plays cruel tricks and now we were battling against the seas in the dreaded Alderney Race, where the tide runs at seven knots. The men put another five rolls in the mainsail, making a total of seven, and still we moved through the rough water at an alarming speed. Sailing fast into the unknown is a terrifying experience, but we were holding the strong tide. We must be doing seven knots. The sea was getting worse. I soon succumbed to seasickness. I went below to help Bunty make some soup, but couldn't stay to finish the job.

It was bitterly cold on deck. I vomited and then took the wheel from John. Philip seemed to have the best ear for judging the position of Alderney. It was all we had to guide us. Every time we asked him the position he replied, 'North-west, it sounds about north-west to me.'

So it continued through the long, cold night. The wind was slightly ahead, so we had to tack several times in order to keep our position in relation to Alderney. Every time we went about I took the wheel as I found the runners and jib sheets too heavy to handle. I hadn't used winches before, and although they were supposed to make things easier, I preferred the old-fashioned block and tackle system used on *Gossip* to these newfangled gadgets. Feet and arms were required to shift the runners and if you weren't very quick with the winches for the jib-sheets, it was impossible to get them in hard enough.

As the night wore on we huddled in the deckhouse for warmth, alert and ready if the helmsman should call us. Bunty was wonderful at looking after us and keeping up our morale. Hot drinks and soup were served almost hourly to those who could swallow them. Sometimes I lay in the scuppers and vomited and sometimes John joined me in my misery but every time we tacked or tended the sails, we all came on duty and worked like automatons taking over our jobs silently and efficiently.

Once as I lay in the scuppers with the waves breaking over me, I missed John. I reached out my hand to see how he was faring. A minute before he had been beside me, and now I realized he had gone. Could he have been swept overboard as he vomited over the side?

'John,' I called.

No answer came, but seconds later a heavy sea shook the ship and he rolled back into the scuppers. I put out my hand again, it was cold and numb, but I felt his body. He was safe. Bunty gave me a hot water bottle, and I tucked it under my oilskins and felt its warm comfort against my unhappy stomach when next I took the wheel.

I struggled to sing some hymns as I steered, and even managed a few verses from Tennyson's

Revenge with quite a strong convincing voice.

Bess was steering at four o'clock, when her shout of 'Land ahead!' roused us to action.

There it was, grim and high, and dead ahead of the advancing yacht. It was so close we could have hit it with a stone. The gulls rose, alarmed at our proximity, squawking as they swerved over the ship.

'Take the helm, Cecily, and gybe her!' shouted Bess.

I took over instantly. The men managed the sheets and runners and the great boom swung across. Suddenly, as we gathered way on the new course, rocks loomed up all round us as the ominous grey cliff was swallowed up in the fog astern.

'Keep a look-out forward, Philip,' ordered Bess. 'I must study the chart.'

The blue-grey rocks stood out in the misty dawn like skulls at Golgotha. They had surely claimed their victims in the past. Wrecked ships as well as human bones must lie at the bottom of the sea. A cold icy hand seemed to guide the ship. Was it mine? Or was it a skeleton hand from one of the inmates of Golgotha? The icy fingers moved down my spine, gripping each vertebra in turn. I shivered, retching from hidden depths, and spewed up yellow bile. So this was Golgotha.

Philip was splendid. He stood before the mast and directed me through the rocks using hand signals. We were right in the midst of them. Sometimes they stuck out grey and menacing. Sometimes the seas broke over them warning of shoals close to the surface. After ten long minutes we seemed to be clear of the reef. Incredible to think that *Sea Jack* had made her own way through these rocks only a short time before. Some hand must have guided her, or perhaps Bess had inherited Dambom's amazing capacity for good luck as well as so many of his mannerisms.

As dawn broke, the fog cleared slightly, and for the first time that night we saw Alderney light. We were now able to judge our position more accurately and

we realized that we had sailed right inside Les
Roches de Jobourg and come within a stone's throw
of the Nez de Jobourg.

We had fought the Race of Alderney for six hours
and remained very much in the same area although
with the wind slightly ahead, we had made a number
of tacks. Now we had conquered. The tide slackened,
and soon we were able to pick out the light on the
Cap de la Hague.

Bess, alarmed now at the sight of the rocks, gave
the point a wide berth, and soon we were swept
eastward by the flood tide in the Channel.

We missed the western entrance to Cherbourg
harbour, and had to come up against the strong tide
before making the eastern entrance between the two
forts. I was steering when we entered the Grande
Rade, or outer harbour. Bess went below to start the
engine, and the men went forward to clear the
halyards ready for handing the sails. Suddenly I
realized something was wrong. The jib rattled down
of its own accord and was caught by the strong wind,
now about Force 7, which whirled it about and
lashed it against the fore-stay.

Sea Jack was so big, and the bowsprit so far away
from me that I didn't realize what had happened.
Bess hurried aft and told me to luff up, as the shackle
pin of the jib purchase had broken and crashed to the
deck, and Philip had to go out on the bowsprit and
retrieve the flapping sail. It was a most unpleasant
job as there was no safety net under him when he
balanced on the spar and un-hooked the hanks of the
jib.

Eventually, all was under control, and the mainsail
came down according to plan. I steered into the yacht
harbour, and we picked up a buoy close to the quay.
It was noon. We had been at sea for twenty-five
hours and all of us had been on duty for every one of
those hours. No wonder that my arms felt incapable
of lifting the heavy mainsail when we tried to make it
up neatly in harbour. They were robot's arms which

had become disconnected from their central
mechanism. They reached up to lift the sail, but I was
no part of them. I watched them, fascinated, as they
worked independently of my impulses. My fingers
moved too, knotting the tyers in place round the
boom. I looked at the rest of the crew, they seemed
all right. Perhaps I was a ghost. John took the other
end of the tyer and we tightened it together. He
didn't seem to realize that my arms were detached
from my body. As a doctor he must often have seen
people wandering on different planes of reality,
unsure of the world in which they were living. He
looked at me strangely, as if from a great distance. I
felt like the Ancient Mariner. I felt I had lived
through a thousand years. But was I alive now, or
was I a ghost?

Bunty roused us by calling out that a meal was
ready. She hadn't known whether to prepare
breakfast or lunch. It didn't matter, no one knew
what time it was, but they were all hungry and did
justice to the good meal she produced.

I sipped some tea, and watched them eating. Was I
a ghost? I was too tired to speculate about it any
longer, and when Bunty refilled my hot water bottle I
took it and retired to my bunk although my legs were
now behaving in a similar manner to my arms, and
made their way across the saloon floor without the
help of my brain to guide them.

Later that evening, when we were all rested and the
others were planning to go ashore for dinner, I asked
Bess how she had managed to survive the long rough
passage without being sick, as she was never a very
good sailor.

'Oh, I was too frightened to be sick,' she said.

So that was the answer. I was too sick to be
frightened - except in Golgotha - and Bess was too
frightened to be sick.

We set the alarm for six o'clock the following
morning, as we were still a long way from Deauville
and time was running out. I filled myself up with

Avomin and Dramamin that day, but we sailed across the bay in the lightest of winds on a calm unruffled sea. The lock-gates were shut when we reached Deauville just after dark, so we passed the gay lights of the Casino and altered course for Le Havre.

At eight-thirty-five we sighted Le Havre light-vessel, and from then on it was a nightmare of flashing lights as we entered the great Seine estuary. Bess studied the chart all the time, and called out the lights which Bunty identified. She was soon adept at telling the occulting from the flashing lights, and very quick at picking out the various coloured lights which we had to get into line. I steered on the given course and the men worked the ship. It was one of the most exciting night sails I have ever done. Bess was splendid and quite unruffled in spite of the heavy traffic working its purposeful way up and down the different channels and mouths of the mighty Seine. It seemed a miracle to me, when, without any mishap or confusion of ways, we dropped our anchor in the 'arrière port' just clear of the Normannia at half past midnight.

At half past five the next morning, we were hailed by the harbour master who told us we hadn't enough water where we were lying, and would ground before low water. Consequently, half an hour later, we were under way, and as we entered the Grande Rade we hoisted the mainsail and foresail and under this rig sailed to Deauville harbour, where we moored *Sea Jack* in her usual berth close to the Yacht Club.

Sailing with Dambom we were apt to take his knowledge and experience for granted. Sailing without him we were very conscious of our ignorance.

This was the first time Bess had sailed as skipper of a yacht, but a few years after this memorable sail she married Lionel, and so became a regular member of *Sea Jack*'s crew.

1956-64 – Solent and the Grandchildren

During the forty-three years in which Dambom owned *Gossip* her life followed a similar annual pattern. The spring period of fitting-out, the long cruise in June and July, during which she might sail 1,000 miles, and the day sails and short cruises in September which always culminated with the Beaulieu Meet. Yacht and skipper must have sailed 40,000 miles together over the years, but although the pattern might well be the same, no two sailing days were ever similar, which is why one never grows tired of the sea.

Living as we did in Yarmouth, we observed everything that moved on the waters of the Solent. Before the war we watched the lovely 'J' class yachts at Cowes, when King George V raced the sleek, black *Britannia* against *Astra*, *Candida*, *Shamrock*

and *Westward*. These lovely ladies never raced after
the war, but new classes sprang up every year and we
watched them make their debut in the Solent.

It was in September 1952 when we first saw the
Princess Flying Boat. We were sailing to Beaulieu
on one of those rare, beautiful days when the sea was
sparkling like sapphires and the sky was the colour
of the blue-winged humming bird. *Gossip was*
drifting with the tide, her sails limp and useless,
when we heard a roar from the sky and as we looked
up the sun flashed on the fuselage of a silver monster
zooming towards us, low on the horizon. As we
watched, the giant alighted, swanlike, with wings
outstretched, and sheets of spray radiated across the
sky, lit by the sun in two iridescent rainbows. The
bird came straight towards us, its six propellers
whirling as though it would attack us and grind us to
a pulp, but it passed by several yards clear of our
bow then, as though it had seen enough of our planet
and our yacht, it rose again and majestically roared
on its way.

Unfortunately, the *Princess* never had the success it
deserved and it was heartbreaking to see this vital
giant lashed down on the hard at Cowes for so many
wasted years like a dragon-fly entangled in the
impregnable web of a spider.

A more successful mode of transport which was
also launched from Cowes was the first hovercraft,
the S.R.N.I., which took us completely by surprise.
We were sailing off Newtown one afternoon early in
the summer of 1959 when this strange object roared
across our bows at a tremendous speed and
disappeared in a cloud of spray. This was our first
view of the ugly but ingenious skimming saucer
riding on its petticoat and we gasped as it thundered
by, half expecting to see little green men popping out
of the hatchway.

In 1958 Dambom decided it was time to take his
three grandchildren, then aged eleven, ten and nine
years old, on their first cruise. They had all learnt to

sail much as we had, by 'messing about in boats', but Graeme was a craftsman as well as a sailor and under his guidance they built their own boats. They started by making rafts which they constructed from driftwood and oil-drums, found after totting on the 'dump'. They worked together in perfect harmony, perhaps because although they were so different in character they all had salt water in their veins.

Graeme was the Master Builder and the recognized leader of the three, whether at sea, or in one of their small camps. James the baby, the scholar and the scribe, greatly admired Graeme's craftsmanship and acted as his devoted apprentice, both in raft-making and in sailing. Susan, at ten years old, was already the busy little housewife cooking and catering for their camping expeditions, and as James once said of his cousin, 'It's nice for us boys having Sue because she makes all our sails.'

Gossip was slightly over-manned on this trip, for with Dambom, Lucia, the three children and myself we were a bunk short. We solved this problem by towing *Jane*, a fourteen-foot Yachting World day boat, which with the aid of an awning, made a possible sleeping cabin for the young and hardy Dillons.

In addition to *Jane* we towed *Bulgy* (*Gossip*'s tender) and on deck we carried James's tiny dinghy *Sea Bear*, which was just big enough to hold the young crew and gave them a certain independence which suited all parties. Fishing rods were smuggled on board and hidden out of sight of Dambom's eagle eye until we were clear of the harbour. He hated the things, having once damaged his toe on an unguarded hook and would have forbidden them if he had spotted them in time.

We sailed to Poole the first day and had a good prawning session in Studland Bay close to Old Harry and his wife - the white chalk guardians of the bay - before anchoring for the night off Brownsea Island. Lucia and I told the children how, years before, when we were about their ages, we had landed on the forbidden beach of this alluring island, and thinking we were unobserved, had dug some good rag-worms for bait before being disturbed by a stentorian voice, issuing from a grim-looking figure on the bank, ordering us to clear off at once. It is said that stolen sweets are best. Certainly those luscious fat worms were the best we ever had, and they were no effort to dig, practically giving them-selves up and walking into our tins.

The children went exploring in *Sea Bear* that first evening while Lucia and I cooked the prawns and prepared dinner and Dambom read a thriller by his favourite author, Ngaio Marsh. His choice of author varied with the years. The first books I remember him reading were the Sherlock Holmes series. These were followed by Sapper's 'Bulldog Drummond' tales and I often succeeded in secreting one of these under my pillow at night so that I too could share the malicious deeds of Carl Peterson before frightening myself into a nightmarish sleep.

After dinner and a spirited game of Ludo, Graeme and Susan collected their sleeping-bags and settled down on *Jane*'s bottom boards while Lucia and I fitted the awning over the little boat making it rain-proof.

It was just after midnight when we were all comfortably settled in our bunks that Lucia and I heard that unmistakable low scrunching, rumbling noise followed by the snag of the anchor chain, a pause, then the rumbling and grumbling again. We looked out of the hatchway and just as we had expected, the trees on Brownsea Island appeared to be moving away from us. 'Dambom!' we shouted, 'Anchor dragging.'

He was with us at once and as he tried to start the engine, Lucia and I took in the spare chain and started to pull in the wayward C.Q.R. anchor. This roused James from his bunk in the fo'c's'le and he emerged from the fore-hatch pulling a heavy sweater over his tousled red curls, excited at the thought of a midnight adventure. Unfortunately we grounded on a sandbank before Dambom could kick the engine into action and then followed a period of drying out and all the discomfiture of lying on our beam-ends. At regular intervals we had to lower the ropes holding *Jane*, as she was in danger of being lifted out of the water as we listed with the falling tide. Nothing disturbed the sleeping occupants, which added to the delight of the youngest member of the crew who reckoned he was scoring over them and having a special treat.

Altogether it was a lively night and it wasn't until well after dawn that we re-floated and were able to start the engine and motor to a new anchorage where we could lie in peace.

Just as Lucia and I were settling down for an hour's sleep before breakfast, we were roused by a shout from on deck.

'Dambom! Dambom, guess what's happened! We're in a different place. *Gossip* must have dragged her anchor in the night while you were asleep!'

After several windy days spent sailing *Jane* in Poole Harbour, rowing in *Sea Bear* and fishing from the deck of *Gossip* with Brownsea Island worms, our little fleet sailed back to Yarmouth for fresh supplies before moving on to the Beaulieu River for the Meet of the Royal Cruising Club.

This is a splendid end-of-season gathering, when all the members foregather in the peaceful reach of the river south of Gin's Farm and discuss their recent cruises.

We sailed up the river on the Thursday evening as Dambom liked to pick his anchorage before the crowd arrived. It was interesting to watch the cream of the cruising world as they sailed up the river, like an invasion fleet, on Friday evening and Saturday morning, as the tides served either from the Hamble or from the west.

Dambom at the helm, 1962.

1958 proved to be a record year with eighty-two yachts anchored in a surprisingly small area. The Commodore's yacht *Restive* formed the nucleus of the fleet with *Dyarchy*, *Blue Bird of Thorne*, *Sandevore* and *Atlantis* all moored alongside her to make a huge floating raft, like Caligula's ill-fated bridge, and the other seventy-seven yachts gathered round as close as possible, like baby chicks trying to get under the wing of the mother hen.

One of the customs at the Meet is for the yachts to fly the flags of all the countries they have visited during their recent cruises. One year, the little yacht *Query*, sailed single-handed by Dick Stevens from

Stockholm to Finland, and back to Yarmouth, was able to display a hoist of seven flags on her starboard cross-trees; and the year the Hiscocks returned from their second world circumnavigation in *Wanderer III*, they had so many flags to show that they dressed their ship overall, with a splendid array of national flags which stretched from stern to stern, so that even the experienced and intrepid members of the Cruising Club 'could scarce forbear to cheer'.

We spent most of Saturday morning visiting our friends in other yachts. Foremost of these was Donald Cree in *Gulnare* where the gin flowed freely and we were always sure of a great welcome and a plethora of amusing stories. The weather deteriorated all the morning and varied between wind and rain squalls and sudden bright sunny intervals. The children made a jury-rig for *Sea Bear* and with the aid of *Gossip*'s table-cloth sailed her before the wind, with considerable danger and excitement. It was gusting at Force 6 or 7 and they were able to sail from *Gossip* to the river-bank - a distance of thirty feet - in a very short time, after which they had to dismantle the sail and row back to the ship. They repeated this performance again and again. It was rather similar to tobogganing, they had to row hard against the wind for the sake of a few brief moments of ecstasy running full tilt with the wind astern.

At six o'clock that evening everyone collected on *Dyarchy* and the raft of boats. Little dinghies came from every yacht and were tied astern in clutches of ten or twelve as the oilskin-clad owners and their crews clambered on board. The yachts sank lower and lower in the water - the boot-tops disappeared like the Plimsoll line on an overloaded cargo ship - and still the people came. Corks popped, champagne flowed, and everyone talked at once. The children, armed with bottles of Coca-Cola, climbed the ratlines, sucking the treacly liquid through straws as they hung like animated monkeys from the rigging. Once, during a faint lull, I heard my small son's voice calling above the chatter at deck level 'Hi Wells mi. What ever are you doing up there?'

I looked up to see Antony Wells, his young prep. school friend, holding on to the cross-trees on one of the other yachts which formed the raft.

In the midst of the celebrations the rain, which had been threatening all the afternoon, descended on the throngs gathered on the decks of the various yachts. Some people sought refuge below, but there wasn't room for many, so we pulled on our sou'westers and oilskins and braved it out. When the time came to leave, the heavens opened and we claimed our water-logged dinghies and rowed off in a veritable cloud-burst.

That evening, when the rain died down, all the children from the different yachts collected their sausages, and barbecued them on the beach with the friendly natives from the Beaulieu River Sailing Club. When we wanted them to come on board again we sent off flares and rockets and all the yachts joined us in a great burst of fire. This was an old custom to signify the end of the festivities and all the nearby lifeboats had been warned in advance.

In 1961 Dambom and the mate celebrated their golden wedding with a great party at Norlands and for the occasion, we commissioned Derek Foster to paint a picture of *Gossip* sailing off the Castle at Cowes.

Gossip went to Brittany as usual that year but she was beginning to feel her age. Dambom found some weakness in the mast when he had it down in the yard but nothing daunted, he just took a few inches off the soft wood from the top and re-adjusted the truck, saying it would last for many more years. A similar weakness was found in the rudder when we did the 'Scrub', but again it only meant cutting out the rotten wood and as Dambom said, 'There's still plenty of rudder left to steer her with.'

Dambom, aged eighty, rigging Gossip.

Both water tanks had given out the previous year
but with a series of Heath Robinson tubes and
contraptions, water could be syphoned from the fore-
tank so we just abandoned the after-tank and made
do with a spare Thomas for washing purposes.

Gossip's engine had always been erratic but this
year, and for ever after, it remained jammed in gear -
there was no neutral and no reverse. When I sailed in
other people's yachts I was amazed at the ease in
which they entered harbour. Standing at the tiller, the
helmsman had only to press a button and the engine
sprang into life and still in the same position he could
control it with the touch of a lever and the yacht

reversed, stopped, or went ahead, and could turn in its own length like a London taxi-cab. Of course one missed half the fun. Entering harbour in *Gossip* was a battle of strength and wits. Dambom always spent a good ten minutes below trying to start the engine, first cranking the handle by hand with his head close to the open bilges, and then when he tired of that he would crank with his bare foot and prehensile toes. As soon as it started he would rush up on deck and take command while one of the crew took over as engineer. Sometimes it would choke and then one had to feed the carburettor with petrol a drop at a time from a cigarette tin until Dambom had time to unscrew the pipe on deck and blow down the twelve-foot petrol pipe.

As we motored up the harbour one of the crew would stand by to catch *Zilla*'s life-rail as we came alongside and another would stand by the spare anchor, which was already in the stern and had to be thrown over if we missed *Zilla* as the bridge was only a few yards from our mooring and presented a real hazard on a flood tide. Everything depended on stopping the engine at the crucial moment when the yacht had just enough way on to reach *Zilla*. The most efficient way of doing this at a moment's notice was to throw Dambom's wet face flannel over the plugs and although this method shocked some of our more mechanical friends, they never suggested a better one.

Leaving the harbour had its difficulties also because once the engine decided to start we had to leave at that precise moment, and as Dambom was sweating away down below he couldn't see if the way was clear, yet go we must, regardless of other craft, or our arms would be pulled out of their sockets as we struggled to hang on.

I remember one day when we were trying to leave St. Peter Port harbour and Mrs. Bibby of *Blue Hills* was holding our warp while Dambom struggled with

the engine. After some time it started so unexpectedly
that no one was on deck and poor Mrs. Bibby was
shouting for help as she held *Gossip*, who was leaping
ahead like a prancing pony on a leading rein.

In 1963 when Dambom was in his eighty-fourth
year we fitted out for the last time. A little more was
taken off the rudder, and a little more was taken off
the mast, otherwise she was just the same with the
same idiosyncratic engine jammed in 'go ahead'.
Gossip sailed west that year but didn't cross the
Channel. We went as usual to the Beaulieu Meet but
when we left after the weekend the engine failed. As
we drifted from our anchorage in a flat calm the tide
caught the yacht and drew her stern first down the
tricky Bull channel (the short cut out of the river).
Luckily Ronald had his outboard engine and by
attaching it to the dinghy we managed to tow *Gossip*
back to the main river. Dambom started the engine at
that moment saying as it spurted into action, 'That's
the last time. The damn thing will never start again,
it's completely seized up.'

Dambom never put *Gossip* up for sale but he was
beginning to feel that the time had come to part with
her, when out of the blue, three Bretons appeared at
Norlands one evening and asked if they could buy
her. He realized that fate had sent them and it seemed
right that *Gossip* should return to her favourite
cruising grounds of Brittany and so it was that a few
weeks later this grand old yacht sailed out of our
lives with a new owner and a new nationality.

Two years later we had news of her from Brittany.
Graeme had to spend a night in St. Malo, while
waiting to join a ship. He booked a room at a small
house on the quay and the owner asked him where he
came from.

'The Isle of Wight,' said Graeme, hoping the
Frenchman had heard of it.

'Oh! Then you must know the yacht *Gossip*,' said
his host.

When Graeme explained that he was Dambom's grandson, he was welcomed into the heart of the family who had all sailed with Monsieur Philip Bozzi in the yacht, which was now berthed at Granville. They were able to tell him that after sixty-five years the spruce mast had been replaced and various alterations had been made down below. They all spoke of her with great affection and it was clear that once again *Gossip* was the centre of a happy family.

In 1969, Desmond noticed an article in the French magazine *Neptune*, written by Monsieur Berthier which throws an interesting light on our old ship. Lionel translated it as follows:

OLD SHIPS - *GOSSIP*

Now that mainly metal or plastic hulls are seen lying alongside our quays, it is indeed rare to find a survivor of the age of sail, without winches. The god Neptune kindly arranged that *Gossip* Philip Bozzi, a real tough hand on a sheet if ever there was one) should come to moor alongside the yacht pontoon in the Bassin Vaubin at St. Malo.

I had the pleasure of going on board for a short cruise to St. Helier in Jersey. What a joy it was for me to appreciate the craftsmanship put into this ancient racing yacht from across the Channel. Indeed *Gossip* was built, like *Firecrest*, by Harris in 1899. Thus, for seventy years, her elegant teak hull has ploughed the waters from Portugal to Norway, including naturally, her native Solent, where Philip discovered her six years ago. The old owner, of eighty-three summers, had not been sailing for two years. His crew, his wife of seventy-two years, could no longer sheet the headsails flat enough for his liking, so he had to separate himself from the boat which they had sailed together for over forty years. If one must admit that the durability of present-day yacht construction is not what it used to be, the same phenomenon appears to

be true of the human race. *Gossip*'s staysail sheet,
without a purchase, was always pulling me along with
it, and I only just avoided being pulled through the
deck fairlead. I clearly felt that the old campaigner,
who a short time ago was wearing the White Ensign
of the Royal Yacht Squadron on her long ensign staff
which hung over her graceful counter, was laughing
gently at me, for my 136 pounds did not weigh much
in the balance.

Her planking must have split open from laughing to
see me squatting on the bobstay, my shoulders
hunched under her enormous bowsprit, trying to
make fast to a mooring buoy, and struggling up over
her varnished hull, my boots full of water.

I must admit that I had not learned to act quickly
enough in a gybe, when thirty fathoms of main sheet
had to be hauled in fast, while the boom, a little spar
thirty feet long, swept low across the deck.

But while there are many things which one cannot
help admiring, the racy elegance of this old boat, her
generous sheer, her bold old-fashioned overhangs,
her solid planked decks (which indeed wept a few
salty tears here and there) on which stood just a small
coach roof, with a couple of varnished skylights, her
outsize gaff cutter rig with jib, staysail, mainsail, and
jack-yard topsail the whole measuring more than
1,000 square feet, one is especially struck by the
finish of the fittings below decks.

The varnished and moulded pitchpine of the
panelling is seen in proximity to the copper of the oil
lamps in gimbals. In the saloon fixed under the
skylight, a brass tell-tale compass swings its
decorated rose over the swinging table, which is so
effective that the boat always appears upright even
after the toughest of races (or after the toughest of
wine sessions). The spacious berths (90 cms) give an
idea of what comfort at sea meant in Great Britain in
the nineteenth century. Even the motor, squeezed
between two massive frames (one pair 12 by 12
spaced every 18 cms for a 34-foot boat. but one

which it is true has a displacement of more than thirteen tons) is itself an antique, and if it often proves to be deaf to the entreaties of the crew, it has a right to be hard of hearing at well over thirty-five years of age, and it always ends by yielding after half an hour on the starting handle.

I think that nowadays it would be impossible to have such a yacht built in the same way, or at the same price, and in any case, wood of that quality is now unobtainable. Let us rejoice that a few of these floating museums are still afloat, even though it is becoming more and more difficult to find any still absolutely intact, as is *Gossip*.

Epilogue

'I must go down to the sea again,
for the call of the running tide
Is a wild call and a clear call
that may not be denied'

J. Masefield

It is good to know that *Gossip* is still sailing in Brittany. Lucia and Desmond saw her lying alongside the quay at Granville early this year. She had changed the colour of her topsides from green to royal blue and looked smart and well cared for. I sometimes wonder if the table-drawer still jams, if the taps are still unconnected to the tanks and if the rows of little golliwogs still adorn the fo'c's'le. She is in her seventy-third year, and Dambom is over ninety, but the sea still calls them both.

Dambom enjoys racing and sailing *Anthea* and once every year he and the mate have their annual sail to the Needles. I can see them now as they walk down the club pier together, Dambom clad in his maroon-coloured shorts rolled up to reveal his thin, muscular legs, scarred and gashed from his hours with the axe, his bare feet gripping the laths of the stage as he carries *Anthea*'s large sail bag on his back. The mate walks beside him, erect as ever, her grey tweed coat and skirt a generous length, her velour hat pulled well down over her hair shading the little opal earrings which dangle as she walks. Her legs are well protected by thick lisle stockings and on her feet I feel sure she is wearing the identical white sand-shoes which she pressed so firmly and steadfastly against the horse of the foresail when, with Cousin Id, she rowed *Gossip* with the giant sweep into Worbarrow Bay so many years ago. She is carrying the lunch in a Spanish wicker basket and I can just see the tip of a bottle peeping out of the top, so I feel sure they are going to toast the Needles in old tawny port, which is all part of the ritual.

Most members hail the club boatman to take them out to their yachts in the launch. Not so Dambom. He is as independent as ever and heaving in the dinghy out-haul he brings *Sea Bear* alongside the steps. Very carefully the mate steps into the tiny boat clutching the basket to her side, and after throwing in the sails - practically on top of her - Dambom takes his seat in the bow of the frail little craft and rows effortlessly out to *Anthea* against the strong tide.

I watch them board the yacht and Dambom is soon at work setting the sails. The mate takes the helm as he casts off the mooring buoy, and just as they are getting under way a little varnished dinghy with a pale blue sail joins them from the harbour and darts hither and thither close beside them like a moth fluttering round a candle. It is Graeme in his Enterprise *Banshee* which he built himself and sailed from Plymouth to Yarmouth, sleeping on the beach beside the boat for two nights on the way. He sails it as if he and the boat were one being and I sometimes think this is just what they are - a sea-centaur, half man and half boat. I am glad he is going to accompany them.

Dambom off to race Anthea *at Cowes, 1969.*

As I watch, the tide catches both the boats, and they are carried westward by the fast running ebb. Soon they are out of sight round the point, but it makes no difference. I know just what they will do. When they reach Alum Bay, Dambom will sail out to thread the Needles. He will gauge the tide so that he clears the rocks beneath his keel, and will chuckle to himself like a recalcitrant schoolboy, as he watches the seas breaking over the hidden shoals when he enters the narrow channel between the venerable chalk sentinels. The cormorants, or Isle of Wight parsons as we call them, will watch for as long as they dare and then they will extend their black swan-like necks and fly away southwards towards France and *Gossip*. The gulls will rise also and beat a noisy retreat, but the brave little puffins, with their comic red beaks, will sit unmoved beside the sleek black and white guillemots on their high chalk ledge and watch *Anthea* as she sails close to the rocks followed by the blue-sailed *Banshee*.

After rounding the Needles lighthouse and acknowledging the friendly waves of the keepers, *Anthea* will sail into Alum Bay and anchor close to the beach so that the mate can watch the 'trippers' as they climb up and down the cliffs collecting the different coloured sands in tiny glass bottles, like a colony of ants working desperately hard at an inexplicable enterprise.

As soon as they are safely anchored Graeme will sail up alongside and join them for lunch. Then Dambom will open his bottle of old tawny port and when all three glasses are pruned he will propose the toast:

'To the Needles'.

I must go down to the sea again,
To the vagrant gypsy life,
To the gull's way and the whale's way
Where the wind's like a whetted knife;
And all I ask is a merry yarn
From a laughing fellow-rover,
And quiet sleep and a sweet dream
When the long trick's over.

J. Masefield

Postscript

Gossip Returns To Yarmouth –
A Last Farewell

It was on a tranquil evening, towards the end of August in 1977, when the shrill ring of my telephone shattered the peace.

'David Lord from the boatyard,' said an eager voice as I picked up the receiver. 'You'll never guess who's just come in the harbour.'

I mentioned the names of several of my friends who were apt to sail into Yarmouth from time to time.

'No,' said David. 'You're not even warm. I shall have to tell you. It's *Gossip*.'

'Thanks,' I said with some incredulity and jammed down the phone without asking for further details. Bursting with excitement I rang my sisters Bess and Jay (Lucia) and my brother Alan. Then I hurried down to the quay where we kept *Bulgy* our old clinker-built dinghy.

We converged, all four of us, simultaneously from our nearby homes. We were all talking at once, no one listening to anyone else, as Alan launched the dinghy and we pushed off from the quay. I noticed that Alan had had the forethought to bring a bottle of champagne and I had a copy of the biography I had written of *Gossip* secreted in my sailing bag.

Gossip was back. *Gossip*, which had been our family yacht for nearly 50 years. We had seen her last in 1964 when my father sold her to two young Bretons. She was 65 years old at the time, now she must be 78, quite an old lady of the sea.

As Alan rowed us across the harbour I thought of that evening thirteen years ago. I remembered *Gossip* as she sailed out of the harbour on a soft autumn afternoon, the sun lighting her varnished mast - a dark green yacht; gaff-rigged and sturdy, all her white canvas set. At her mast head, instead of the familiar burgee of the Royal Cruising Club, had fluttered 'a banner with a strange device' and over her long, counter stern the tri-colour of France. We had all watched her from the quay that day with my father, Dambom, who was then in his 84th year. None of us had spoken. It was a moment in our lives when words meant nothing.

'*Gossip* ahoy,' called Alan, waking me out of my reverie as he pulled up alongside the familiar green yacht, now wearing the French Ensign.

A tall young man slithered down the mast and a smell of fried mackerel wafted up from below. The young man, clad in jeans and a striped tee-shirt, greeted us from the deck.

'William Borel,' he said, holding out a hand in welcome. 'Come aboard.'

'*Gossip* used to belong to us,' said Alan, and we've come to welcome her back.' He produced the champagne as we clambered over the gunwale in our enthusiasm to see our old ship.

Gossip is no longer ours I thought as I stood on deck. She must now be classed as 'other people's boats'.

As we shook hands with William, in true French style, an attractive girl emerged from the fore-hatch.

'This is my crew, Juliette,' said William and as she greeted us a couple from another gaff-rigged cutter, moored alongside, joined the party and were introduced by William as his sailing partners who had cruised with him from Brittany.

'Let's open the champagne,' said William, 'this is a great occasion.'

As we drank to *Gossip* tongues were unloosed, luckily for us mostly in English.

'I only bought her eighteen months ago,' William told us, 'and since then I have spent every weekend working on her. She was in a sorry state as her last owner had neglected her and the yard at St. Malo, where she is based, condemned her as irreparable;

but with the encouragement of my friends and my
own faith in the boat I am bringing her back to life.
This is my first cruise and I wanted to come to
Yarmouth so that I could meet her English owner
and learn all I could about her early days; I want to
get her back to her original state. It is an honour and
a great pleasure for me to have you all aboard.'

This seemed to be my moment. I handed William
my book telling him that my father had died the
previous year, at the age of 96, but that *Gossip*'s life
history was recorded in her biography.

William was delighted with the gift, saying that he
was a journalist photographer and soon we were
opening more wine and planning another book – well
illustrated of course – in which we would combine to
write of the further exploits of *Gossip*.

'I knew I had made no mistake in *Gossip*'s
genealogy,' said William. 'Because as soon as we
came in here the Harbour Master approached us,
stroked her top sides and said:

'*Gossip* is back.'

After a second bottle of French wine had been
consumed William asked if would like to look round.
We had been waiting for this moment ever since we
came on board and soon we were running wild over
our beloved yacht, talking to each other, to our new
French friends or just muttering to ourselves as we
exclaimed with joy that nothing that really mattered
had been changed. Certainly conditions down below
had deteriorated as William's work of restoration had
been concentrated on the essential construction and
safety of the actual hull and spars. It was still
habitable but weeks of work were needed before it
could hope to attain its former state.

The lovely mahogany panelling looked stark and
scarified resembling the unkempt coat of a neglected
Siamese cat but I was glad to see the 'looking lamps'
still sat in their ornate brass holders. I remembered
how it always seemed to be my job to refill them
with paraffin every morning; check the wicks and

clean the delicate globes with tissue paper. No matter
how careful we were they always seemed to have a
black smear and as spares were hard to come by it
was a terrible crime to break one.

The saloon seats had gaping holes in the corded
coverings, which Dambom had made one winter,
revealing the coarse horse hair stuffing. I sat down
gingerly. Yes. It was just as hard as I remembered it
when I had slept there.

Curiously I reached out and gave a slight tug on the
table drawer where we used to keep our cutlery. That
too hadn't changed. It was still jammed. Dambom
always said he would fix it so that it could be opened
without using brute force – but he never had, nor, it
seemed had any of *Gossip*'s owners since his time.

I went next into the fo'c's'le. The half cooked
mackerel had been removed from the blue-flame
stove on our arrival nut the aroma remained recalling
the days when we had caught our own fish and fried
them in the confined space of the galley, sitting on
the paint locker, with our feet on the chain store in
the bilge. I noted that a plastic bucket had replaced
our famous 'Thomas' – an iron bucket which became
our family totem – but the water pump still failed to
work and as in our day the water was stored in a five
gallon drum lashed on a shelf and drawn off by
means of a syphon.

I felt a certain poignancy when I looked into the
open crockery cupboard, known euphemistically as
the pantry, and saw the row of little paper golliwogs
which had been stuck along the top by Dambom's
grandchildren as, day by day, they ate their way
through pot after pot of golden shred marmalade and
strawberry jam.

I heard a noise behind me and looked back to see
Jay grovelling amongst the potatoes in the vegetable
locker.

'What on earth are you up to?' I asked.

'Just looking to see if the hole is still there where
Rufous the hamster gnawed his way through. Yes,

it's there all right. I'll never forget that night when he escaped and we heard him champing away and couldn't reach him because he had got beyond the locker. He would have worked his way right through the ship's side if we hadn't enticed him back with a carrot.'

'I see my cot bunk is still there,' said Alan joining us in the fo'c's'le. 'The canvas looks a bit worn but I expect it would still bear me.'

Before returning to our host I inspected the after-cabin. Shamelessly I opened the sail-locker at the end of one of the bunks. It was full of sails now but I remembered the day, when I was six years old; the day when Dambom bought *Gossip* and sailed her into Yarmouth harbour.

Bess and I, who had been watching her long awaited entry, while standing on the bridge with our nurse, had been taken aboard and after examining everything, much as we were doing now, we had discovered that if we burrowed through the sail-locker we would eventually emerge on deck.

After completing my tour I came up the companionway in time to hear Jay who had spent her honeymoon on *Gossip*, remarking to William that he had made a wise move in changing the transparent glass of the sky-light in the after-cabin to opaque glass – 'for wedding nights' she added unnecessarily.

On deck things were much the same. The sturdy old capstan commanded the foredeck where I had knelt behind Dambom, so many, many times, hauling in the chain as he turned the handle to raise the anchor. Often it had been muddy and I would have to brush it and sluice it with sea water before guiding it down the fair lead to the chain locker in the fo'c's'le. The wooden blocks were all in place but they lacked the golden hue which always radiated from them, each spring, after Dambom had scraped and varnished them.

I was glad to see the mast had been replaced for, during her latter days in Yarmouth, Dambom had

had to remove a portion of the 65 year old spar as a slow rot had set in. I hoped that a new rudder had been fitted for I remembered on the last 'Great Scrub' that part of that essential piece of equipment had been cut away as the same trouble had affected the wood, but as Dambom remarked in his optimistic way;

'There's still enough mast to hold the sails and enough rudder to steer her by.'

As we reassembled on the deck, each with our own special memories, we realised that our new French friends must be longing to eat their half-cooked mackerel, so, after signing the visitor's book we took our leave.

'Come and sail with us tomorrow,' said William as he helped us into *Bulgy*. 'We are going up to Cowes before crossing to St. Malo.'

'We'd love to,' we chorused. 'Au revoir and many thanks.'

Jay, Alan and I turned up the following morning, a little before the arranged time in case *Gossip* slipped away early. We were soon under-way with an engine which hummed reassuringly and was certainly an improvement on the one that had actually died on us in the Bull channel as we left the Beaulieu river on our final sail. I was asked to take the wheel, as we left the harbour, while William and Alan hoisted the mainsail and foresail and unrolled the jib. The wind was a good force 7, probably gusting to 8. I was in my element, splashed with spray by the choppy waters of the Solent, as the boys rolled in three reefs and we beat towards Cowes against a westerly gale with a fair tide beneath our keel. No other boat I had sailed in compared with *Gossip* in these conditions and, as I sat on the steering-locker, grasping the familiar wheel, I was back in the old days. I was fourteen years old, imagining *Gossip* was my horse and I was steering her through the bubbling maelstrom that surged and thundered round the Naze of Norway as we made our treacherous passage to the Hardanger Fjord.

William's friends, in the smaller gaff-rigged cutter, pounded away to leeward, dipping their abnormally long bowsprit into the oncoming waves.

Jay divided up the quiche she had made and we munched hungrily as we tacked outside Gurnard Ledge.

In spite of the head wind we reached Cowes in fairly good time and soon the two boats were moored alongside the jetty, their twin tri-colours adding a continental touch to the old port.

As we drank wine, in the comfort of the saloon, listening to the wind outside, pleasant smells drifted towards us from the galley of the other yacht and soon her crew joined us bearing a Quimper of cold meats and spiced sausage served with a well dressed salad, flavoured with garlic. By the time coffee and Calvados were produced we were all the best of friends.

William told us that he had many plans for *Gossip*'s future once she was fully restored to her former state and, before we left, he and I had already laid the foundations for a new book and he promised to return to Yarmouth every summer so that we could keep in touch.

Régates Née *Gossip*

I had further news of *Gossip* in January, the following year, when William Borel reported the progress he had made during his week-ends working on his boat.

'She is now a good cruising yacht,' he wrote, 'but I have ambition for her. Next November my country is organising the 'Route du Rhum', the first French single-handed race across the Atlantic and I have the 'grande idée', which is to enter *Gossip* for this event.

I have learnt, recently, that she is the sister-ship of the celebrated *Firecrest* in which Alain Gerbault made the first single-handed Atlantic crossing from east to west in 1923 before sailing round the world. Now 55 years later, I hope to do the same. I will have to get a sponsor for the event as, in spite of the work I have already done, there are many things I need before the yacht will qualify to enter the race. I will let you know as soon as I have any news, meanwhile, please tell me what you think of my idea.'

I wrote back with enthusiasm. Of course *Gossip* could do it and I wished him good luck in finding a sponsor.

It was early in May when I heard from William again.

'I have good news,' he wrote. 'The yachting magazine has promised to sponsor me for the 'Route du Rhum'. I am very happy with all the improvements which include an automatic pilot, some fine bronze winches, new sails, a radio transmitter and many other essentials demanded by the rules of the contest. The only condition is that *Gossip* will have to change her name to *Régates* for the period of the race. It is an unlucky thing to do but it has to be. More good news is that I have found a publisher for my book on the story of the race and for this I ask your help for details of 'Father Dambom' and of the fabulous story of *Gossip*.'

He ended by saying that he would bring *Régates* to Yarmouth in August to present us with her new face lift and to invite us all to sail in her once more. He added, as a post script, that she would still bear our racing flag as a memento of our family. I was glad of this. I remembered when Bess made this flag for *Gossip* for the first 'Round the Island Race' in 1931. It depicted Thomas who became the ship's mascot.

Thomas was our bucket – blue on a yellow background for the flag. He was really christened by Dambom in a mistaken belief that it was Sir Thomas Moore (and not Sir John) who was buried 'at dead of night'. It is a rule in various ports that no refuse may be tipped into the harbour. This can prove a problem for yachtsmen whose gash buckets are filled to bursting and so the natural, if undesirable, outcome was that 'Thomas' was discharged at dead of night.

We were all very excited by the thought of *Gossip* – or *Régates* – embarking on this great enterprise, when she would be competing against the elite of the French yachtsmen and immediately made plans to book berths on the Brittany Ferries to St. Malo so that we could watch the start of the 'Route du Rhum'.

With the coming of August there was a great sadness which shattered all our hopes and plans. instead of seeing our old yacht sailing into Yarmouth harbour with all her grand, new gadgets there came a brief letter from William written this time in his native language:

> 'Chère Cecile
> C'est avec beaucoup de tristesse
> Que je vous écris cette lettre –
> *Gossip* est mort.'

Through a mist of tears I tried to read the unfamiliar language. I managed to discern a few brief sentences: 'l'allumage du moteur – à essence' – 'J'étais miraculeusement sauve par un pêcheur.' It was enough. I realised that *Gossip* was dead. She had gone up in flames and William had been saved by a fisherman.

I took the letter to my brother-in-law for a full interpretation and learnt that, within three days of his terrible experience, William had written to me so that he could break the news before I read of the tragedy in the paper.

It was not until August 1979, exactly a year later, that I knew the details of *Gossip*'s sad end. William

sent me a copy of 'Les cahiers du Yachting' in which
he had written an article entitled:

'Vie et mort de mon bateau.'

In some 3,000 words William told the story of 79
years of the life of a cruising yacht. After describing
Gossip in detail he gave a summary of the 44 years
in which Dambom had owned her, as taken from my
book 'The Biography of a Yacht'. He then wrote of
the two years he had spent in fitting and repairing her
after her sojourn in the South of France and finally
he came to his own special story, the ending of the
saga of a much loved ship.

'*Gossip* est mort'
Gossip is dead.

On August 21ˢᵗ 1978, William Borel sailed in
Régates – née *Gossip* – from Camaret, in Brittany,
on a 600 mile single-handed project in order to
qualify for the 'Route du Rhum'. At first all went
well. *Gossip* sailed on a broad reach with a Force 3-4
wind and the Atom self-steering gear working well.
After sweeping through the Raz de Sein, at 7 knots,
he set a course for Spain. That night he realised the
Atom was inadequate to control the yacht's 13 tons
and some hours later, after spending a night at the
helm, he decided to make for Benodet to have it
repaired.

The wind dropped and after 12 hours flopping in a
lifeless sea he decided to start the engine as he
reckoned he had just enough petrol aboard for the
passage to Benodet. Immediately there was a loud
explosion, a hellish blast and *Gossip* was ablaze.
From the motor aft to the stern everything was
burning. William set off a fire-extinquisher - but it
was of no avail. The second one also failed to quell
the flames. The white powder was useless. Buckets
of water only seemed to spread the flames and down

below the smoke made breathing almost impossible. The fire reached the saloon as William plunged below to get the pyrotechric flares and a kitchen knife with which to cut the lashings on the life raft. Seeing the sextant case nearby he picked it up and chucked in an ash tray. Why? He didn't know. He knew only that unaided he couldn't put out the fire and he had to reach the deck before he suffocated. He clawed his way up the companionway and attached the painter of the life-raft to a cleat and threw the raft overboard. Stupefied he watched as it failed to inflate. He hauled it back on deck and noticed, after looking through the hole made for the painter, that the stainless steel cable which worked the compressed air bottle had broken at the neck. He was in a desperate state. He was at least fifty miles from the nearest land and the whole ship was now ablaze. As the terylene sails melted and dripped on the deck and the deck paint hissed and bubbled under his feet, William turned to his flares.

It would be even worse down below I thought, as I read of the horrors William was witnessing and I shared his despair. What could he do. I imagined how the flames would engulf the lovely mahogany panelling in the saloon – the panelling I had polished with such care so many years ago. In the after-cabin too, the wooden bunks would be alight, charring the ceiling we had painted white, lying on the bunks and reaching up with our dripping brushes as we prepared it for Jay's honeymoon.

William sent off two smoke-flares and six red, hand flares which lit up the sea around the burning yacht, but there was no sign of a ship on the wide horizon and he had little hope of them being sighted. Next he sent off four parachute flares hoping they would be seen from a distance but not one of them worked as it should. The second one, instead of soaring 6 metres into the air, went the opposite way and hit his foot, but the pain went unheeded in the stress of the moment.

There was nothing more he could do. *Gossip* had been burning for 30 minutes and now he could only wait. For what was he waiting? He didn't know. He sat on the capstan in the bow. I could picture him there as I read his tale. His last stand was on the stalwart stone block which had wound up the anchor so many hundreds of times when *Gossip* was our yacht. Now its work was over and it would go down with the ship joining lost anchors it had once helped to raise. I know how desperate he must have been feeling both for the loss of his prized boat, and now for his own life.

He watched, half mesmerised, as the new bronze winches disappeared one after another as they fell through the deck which could no longer support them. The fire was everywhere. Flames, a metre high, were spurting through the hatches. He waited in anticipation for the moment when the gas bottles would explode. That would herald the end. He wanted to stay aboard as long as his boat remained afloat.

Suddenly, after scanning the horizon in an almost despairing way, he saw a trawler, about a quarter of a mile off, speeding towards him. As she approached *Gossip* she had to lie off as the flames were horrific. William yelled to the skipper to keep clear on account of the gas bottles and clad in his life jacket he went overboard by the net under the bowsprit still clutching his sextant.

He swam towards the bow of the trawler which towered above him as he struggled to reach her. She seemed to get bigger and bigger and was pitching so much that he felt he might be submerged but he managed to brandish his sextant case at the crew who were stretching out their arms trying to save him. Finally, with a great heave, he found himself on the deck of the fishing boat.

'Don't worry young man,' said one of the crew. 'I've been sunk five times.'

They poured glasses of red wine down his throat, undressed him and fitted him out in over-large seaman's kit.

Once he was safely aboard, the *Santa-Helena*, his rescue ship, approached as near as possible to the burning inferno as the crew plied their fire hoses. But already there was no deck and with a sudden explosion the gas cylinders burst and the fire blazed up once more.

By this time another trawler, *La Jonque*, had seen the flares and broadcasted the alarm. A warship and a helicopter answered the call and were soon on the scene. *La Jonque* tried in vain to extinguish the flames but it was too late. *Gossip* was sinking. The heat of the fire had melted all the skin-fittings. The water was rising.

Before disappearing completely *Gossip* gave a final spasm of vitality. A last agonised death throe. The long counter stern rose in the air; the bowsprit plunged into the sea and slowly she shank.

On August 14th at 18:45 hours in 47° 43N and 5° 10W, the track of the mast which carried *Gossip*'s house-flag – was the last part of the ship to disappear, so that she carried Thomas, our family emblem, with her as she went down.

William wrote:

'Even if such an end is better than being eaten by worms in a mud berth, it was, to my way of thinking, premature – and above all unfair.'

My feelings were much the same. My sisters thought it preferable that *Gossip* should end in such a way rather that become derelict and forgotten in a down-market shipyard but I felt, as William did, that as *Régates* she was just entering into a second life. She was about to embark on the 'Route du Rhum'. She had a young, ambitious owner who had rejuvenated her and built her up, from the neglected state in which he had found her, into a well equipped yacht of which he was justifiably proud.

She may have been classed under 'other people's boats' when she met her tragic end but to me, in a strange way and in my own thoughts, she was still our own *Gossip* sailing under our special flag.

Whenever I sail now, in the vicinity of Ushant, I think of her poor charred hull being swept up and down, by the strong tides, as she haunts the Brittany coast, the ghost of a much loved ship plying the depths of one of her favourite sailing grounds.

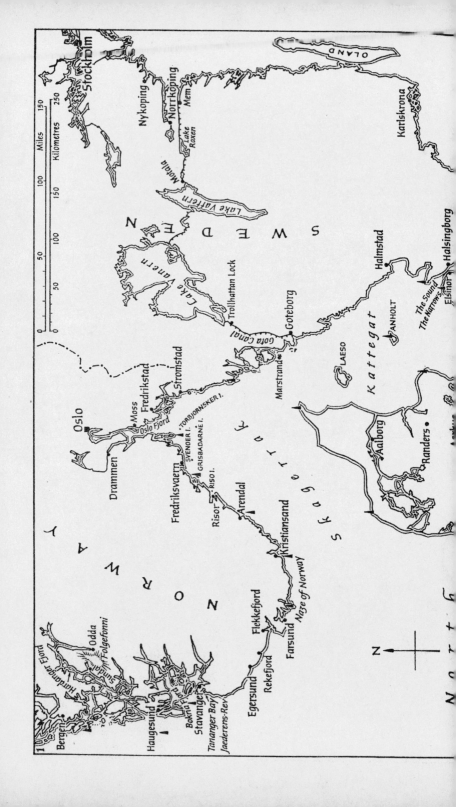

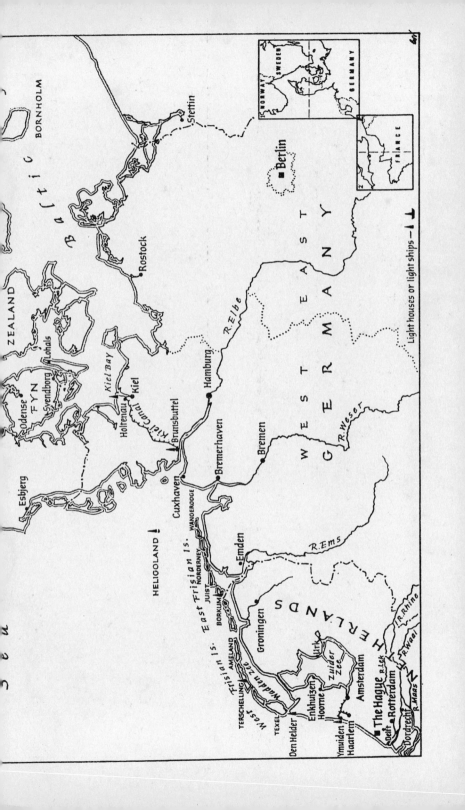

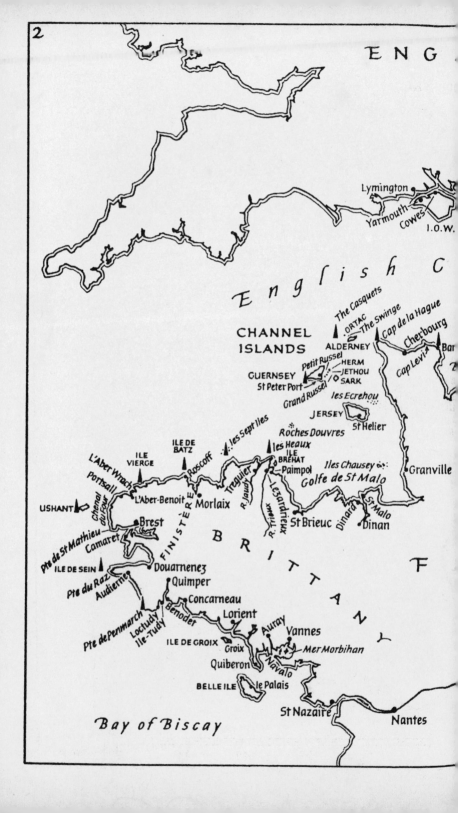

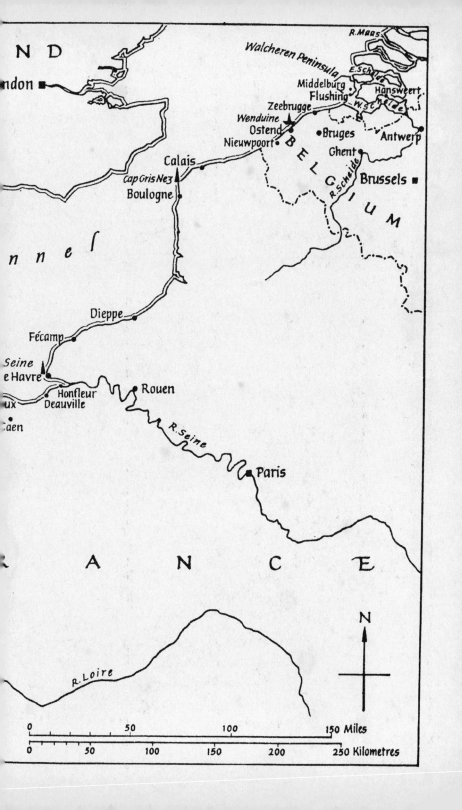